The Language of Love

Anne Harvey writes and broadcasts for radio, and lectures and presents literary programmes and poetry readings at arts festivals and for schools. Anne has edited over thirty anthologies of poetry and drama and in 1992 she was winner of the Signal Poetry Award. In 2004 she was made a Fellow of the Society of Speech and Drama for her lifetime's work in Drama and Literature.

The Language of Love

Poems chosen by
Anne Harvey

MACMILLAN CHILDREN'S BOOKS

First published 1989 by Blackie and Son Ltd

Published 2005 by Macmillan Children's Books
This edition published 2006 by Macmillan Children's Books
a division of Macmillan Publishers Limited
20 New Wharf Road, London N1 9RR
Basingstoke and Oxford
www.panmacmillan.com

Associated companies throughout the world

ISBN-13: 978-0330-41572-9
ISBN-10: 0-330-41572-7

contents

Love Is . . .   1

First Love   9

In Love   39

Love Tokens   95

Love and Marriage   127

Out of Love   161

Lost Love   191

Last Love   213

Index of first lines   227

Index of authors   235

Acknowledgements   239

A Birthday

My heart is like a singing bird
   Whose nest is in a watered shoot;
My heart is like an apple-tree
   Whose boughs are bent with thickset fruit;
My heart is like a rainbow shell
   That paddles in a halcyon sea;
My heart is gladder than all these
   Because my love is come to me.

Raise me a dais of silk and down;
   Hang it with vair and purple dyes;
Carve it in doves and pomegranates,
   And peacocks with a hundred eyes;
Work it in gold and silver grapes,
   In leaves and silver fleur-de-lys;
Because the birthday of my life
   Is come, my love is come to me.

Christina Rossetti

Love Is . . .

love is . . .

love is more thicker than forget
more thinner than recall
more seldom than a wave is set
more frequent than to fail

it is most mad and moonly
and less it shall unbe
than all the sea which only
is deeper than the sea

love is less always than to win
less never than alive
less bigger than the least begin
less little than forgive

it is most sane and sunly
and more it cannot die
than all the sky which only
is higher than the sky

e e cummings

love is . . .

Love is a circle that doth restless move
In the same sweet eternity of love.

Robert Herrick

Love

It is to be all made of sighs and tears . . .
It is to be all made of faith and service . . .
It is to be all made of fantasy,
All adoration, duty and observance,
All humbleness, all patience, all impatience
All purity, all trial, all obedience . . .

William Shakespeare

from Song

Some say that love's a little boy,
    And some say it's a bird,
Some say it makes the world go round,
    And some say that's absurd,
And when I asked the man next-door,
    Who looked as if he knew,
His wife got very cross indeed,
    And said it wouldn't do.

Does it look like a pair of pyjamas,
    Or the ham in a temperance hotel?
Does its odour remind one of llamas,
    Or has it a comforting smell?
Is it prickly to touch as a hedge is,
    Or soft as eiderdown fluff?
Is it sharp or quite smooth at the edges?
    Or tell me the truth above love.

When it comes, will it come without warning
    Just as I'm picking my nose?
Will it knock on my door in the morning,
    Or tread in the bus on my toes?
Will it come like a change in the weather?
    Will its greeting be courteous or rough?
Will it alter my life altogether?
    O tell me the truth above love.

W. H. Auden

Love is Like a Dizziness

O, Love, love, love!
    Love is like a dizziness;
It winna let a poor body
    Gang about his biziness!

James Hogg

Love Is . . .

Love is feeling cold in the back of vans
Love is a fanclub with only two fans
Love is walking holding paintstained hands
Love is

Love is fish and chips on winter nights
Love is blankets full of strange delights
Love is when you don't put out the light
Love is

Love is the presents in Christmas shops
Love is when you're feeling Top of the Pops
Love is what happens when the music stops
Love is

Love is white panties lying all forlorn
Love is a pink nightdress still slightly warm
Love is when you have to leave at dawn
Love is

Love is you and love is me
Love is a prison and love is free
Love's what's there when you're away from me
Love is . . .

Adrian Henri

What Is Love?

Now what is love, I pray thee tell?
It is that fountain and that well
Where pleasure and repentance dwell.
It is perhaps that sauncing bell
That tolls all into heaven or hell:
And this is love, as I hear tell.

Yet what is love, I pray thee say?
It is a work on holy day.
It is December matched with May,
When lusty bloods in fresh array
Hear ten months after of the play:
And this is love, as I hear say.

Yet what is love, I pray thee sain?
It is a sunshine mixed with rain.
It is a toothache, or like pain;
It is a game where none doth gain;
The lass saith No, and would full fain:
And this is love, as I hear sain.

Yet what is love, I pray thee show?
A thing that creeps, it cannot go;
A prize that passeth to and fro;
A thing for one, a thing for mo;
And he that proves must find it so;
And this is love, sweet friend, I trow.

Sir Walter Raleigh

First Love

Taking the Plunge

One day a boy said to a girl in a swimming pool
'I'm going to dive in, are you?' She replied
'No thanks. I bet you can't anyway.' So the boy
got on the diving board and dived and said
'See.' The girl replied 'Flipping eck!'
(Simon Wilkinson, Margaret Wix Junior School, St Albans)

Flipping eck, cor blimey, strewth,
You're my hero, that's the honest truth.

Lummy, crickey, lordy lord,
It's a long way down from that diving board.

Itchy beard and stone the crows,
Don't you get chlorine up your nose?

Luv a duck and strike me pink,
You're slicker than the soap in the kitchen sink.

Knock me down with a sparrow's feather,
How about us going out together?

Groovy, t'riffic, brill and smashing,
Me 'n' you, we could start things splashing.

Watcha cocky, tara, see ya,
Meet me for a coke in the cafeteria.

Hallelujah and Amen,
If you like this poem you can read it again.

John Mole

Prayer for a Cotton Blouse

. . . . and God, bless Carmel Piper
and make her come to Frodsham pretty soon.

You see, the only time I met her,
at Barbara's birthday party
when none of the other boys turned up,

I felt strange with all those ribbons,
lace frills when they curtseyed,
the cake that tasted like church,

And I really had to go now
but she whispered in the hallway
that my socks looked very nice.

Her elbows smelled of lemons
and the bones of her shoulders
were faint beneath her cotton blouse.

She lingered by the door
but my hands were in my pockets
forgive me, Lord.

Dear Lord, I've been so silly.
Make her come to Frodsham
and wear her cotton blouse.

Bless worms, O God, and frogs, and don't forget
the spiders in the coalshed near the door.

John Latham

Indoor Games Near Newbury

In among the silver birches winding ways of tarmac
  wander
And the signs to Bussock Bottom, Tussock Wood and
  Windy Brake,
Gabled lodges, tile-hung churches, catch the lights of
  our Lagonda
As we drive to Wendy's party, lemon curd and
  Christmas cake.
Rich the makes of motor whirring, past the pine-
  plantation purring
          Come up, Hupmobile, Delage!
Short the way your chauffeurs travel, crunching over
  private gravel
          Each from out his warm garage.

Oh but Wendy, when the carpet yielded to my indoor
  pumps
There you stood, your gold hair streaming, handsome
  in the hall-light gleaming
There you looked and there you led me off into the
  game of clumps
Then the new Victrola playing and your funny uncle
  saying

'Choose your partners for a fox-trot! Dance until its
  tea o'clock!
'Come on, young 'uns, foot it featly!' Was it chance
  that paired us neatly,
I, who loved you so completely,
You, who pressed me closely to you, hard against your
  party frock?

'Meet me when you've finished eating!' So we met and
  no one found us
Oh that dark and furry cupboard while the rest played
  hide and seek
Holding hands our two hearts beating in the bedroom
  silence round us
Holding hands and hardly hearing sudden footsteps,
  thud and shriek
Love that lay too deep for kissing – 'Where is Wendy?
  Wendy's missing!'
Love so pure it *had* to end,
Love so strong that I was frighten'd when you gripped
  my fingers tight and
Hugging, whispered 'I'm your friend.'

Good-bye Wendy! Send the fairies, pinewood elf and
   larch tree gnome,
Spingle-spangled stars are peeping at the lush Lagonda
   creeping
Down the winding ways of tarmac to the leaded lights
   of home.
There, among the silver birches, all the bells of all the
   churches
Sounded in the bath-waste running out into the frosty
   air.
Wendy speeded my undressing, Wendy is the sheet's
   caressing
      Wendy bending gives a blessing,
Holds me as I drift to dreamland, safe inside my
   slumberwear.

John Betjeman

The Ballad of Chocolate Mabbie

It was Mabbie without the grammar school gates.
And Mabbie was all of seven.
And Mabbie was cut from a chocolate bar.
And Mabbie thought life was heaven.

The grammar school gates were the pearly gates,
For Willie Boone went to school.
When she sat by him in history class
Was only her eyes were cool.

It was Mabbie without the grammar school gates
Waiting for Willie Boone.
Half-hour after the closing bell!
He would surely be coming soon.

Oh, warm is the waiting for joys, my dears!
And it cannot be too long.
Oh, pity the little poor chocolate lips
That carry the bubble of song!

Out came the saucily bold Willie Boone.
It was woe for our Mabbie now.
He wore like a jewel a lemon-hued lynx
With sand-waves loving her brow.

It was Mabbie alone by the grammar school gates.
Yet chocolate companions had she:
Mabbie on Mabbie with hush in the heart.
Mabbie on Mabbie to be.

Gwendolyn Brooks

First Love

When I was in my fourteenth year,
And captain of the third eleven,
I fell in love with Guenevere,
And hovered at the gate of heaven.
She wasn't more than twenty-seven.

I partnered her, by happy chance,
At tennis, losing every game.
No shadow dimmed her careless glance,
No teasing word, no hint of blame,
Brightlier burned my secret flame.

Nothing I asked but to adore,
No dumb surrender, shy and stiff:
But ah, she gave me how much more,
A benison beyond belief!
'Just hold my racquet for a jiff.'

Gerald Bullett

Thelma

Thelma was a Brownie,
I never spoke to her
Although we spent a year together
In Standard Three.
I once followed her home
From the Brownie HQ.
There was honeysuckle in the gardens;
Songs of gramophones, too.
The satchel she brought to school
Was made of expensive leather
And in her hair
She wore a slide of tortoiseshell
My first fetish.
We never spoke,
Not once in all that time.
It was a long spell
And is not over:
When I smell honeysuckle now
It is Thelma I smell.

Vernon Scannell

Salcombe (1948)

Oh I remember how the sea
Came washing to our feet
That morning
And how my mother chanced to meet
Your mother
And father dozed in the August heat
And the gulls cried.

And how you said your name was Anne
And how my sister teased
Your cousin
And how your dog played as he pleased
In the waves
And barked and shook himself and sneezed
And the band played.

And how amongst the parasols and feet
We dug beneath the strand
A tunnel
And how my fingers wet with sand
Suddenly
Broke through and touched your stranger's hand
And the world turned.

Gareth Owen

Who else can make me feel like I'm handsome and tall
Who else can make me feel I'm on top of it all
I've found a combination that works like a charm
I'm simply a man who walks on the stars
Whenever it's Anne on my arm . . .

Jerry Herman

Sonnet

I wish I could remember that first day,
First hour, first moment of your meeting me,
If bright or dim the season, it might be
Summer or Winter for aught I can say;
So unrecorded did it slip away,
So blind was I to see and to foresee,
So dull to mark the budding of my tree
That would not blossom yet for many a May.
If only I could recollect it, such
A day of days! I let it come and go
As traceless as a thaw of bygone snow;
It seemed to mean so little, meant so much;
If only now I could recall that touch,
First touch of hand in hand – Did one but know!

Christina Rossetti

A Puddle in the Life of Oscar Summerfield

Ozzie puts his hands in his pockets –
Not just for warmth
But that secure feeling of being whole.
Again he passes walking frowns –
Smiles smuggled safely
In briefcases and purses
And homes in the deepest jungles of suburbia.
Another muddy puddle
Seeps into his plimsoll
(The one with the hole in it
– his polo shoe)
And his toes wriggle
In soggy abstraction
While his mind drifts amongst his life
And the wind ruffles his hair
With fingers imported especially from the North
(Just for him)
And whispers sweet sentiments in his ear
While whipping around behind him
To stab an icicle in his back.

She smiles towards him –
Not at him, but (nevertheless)
Towards him
And her cold blue eyes,
(Sheffield steel)
Flecked with life and beauty,
Search his soul
(Like the mud does his plimsoll)
And her golden charm
Perceives nothing in him
After all,
'Only nutters stand in muddy puddles.'

Barry Weaver

Lizzie Pitofsky Poem

I can't get enoughsky
Of Lizzie Pitofsky
I love her so much that it hurts.
I want her so terrible
I'd give her my gerbil
Plus twenty-two weeks of desserts.

I know that it's lovesky
'Cause Lizzie Pitofsky
Is turning me into a saint
I smell like a rose,
I've stopped picking my nose,
And I practically never say 'Ain't'.

I don't push and shovesky
'Cause Lizzie Pitofsky
Likes boys who are gentle and kind.
I'm not throwing rocks
And I'm changing my socks
(And to tell you the truth I don't mind)

Put tacks in my shoes,
Feed me vinegar juice,
And do other mean, bad, awful stuffsky.
But promise me this:
I won't die without kiss–
ing my glorious Lizzie Pitofsky.

Judith Viorst

Blue Eyes

Barbara Cushion
Weeps in the lane,
And vows she will never
Go brambling again.

Down her fat face
Fat teardrops run,
And splash on her bosom,
One by one.

With sobs and cries
She shakes like a shape –
What is the matter,
Is it a rape?

Oh no! It's her feelings,
Poor girl, that smart;
And Jem's unkindness
Has broken her heart.

For months she has had
A mind to Jem,
So when she was out
She smiled at him;

Down the green lane
She watched him come –
But all he did
Was to pinch her bum.

Sylvia Townsend Warner

First Love

I ne'er was struck before that hour
    With love so sudden and so sweet.
Her face it bloomed like a sweet flower
    And stole my heart away complete.
My face turned pale as deadly pale,
    My legs refused to walk away,
And when she looked 'what could I ail?'
    My life and all seemed turned to clay.

And then my blood rushed to my face
    And took my sight away.
The trees and bushes round the place
    Seemed midnight at noonday.
I could not see a single thing,
    Words from my eyes did start;
They spoke as chords do from the string
    And blood burnt round my heart.

Are flowers the winter's choice?
   Is love's bed always snow?
She seemed to hear my silent voice
   And love's appeal to know.
I never saw so sweet a face
   As that I stood before:
My heart has left its dwelling-place
   And can return no more.

John Clare

The Girl's Confession

He loves me for imagined excellences
I never owned or claimed:
Not least for my body, whose upkeep is costly
And whose movements are others', carefully mimed.

He is unaware of the irony,
As he was of the preparation, the endless preening;
The hours before the mirror; the slow walk
With books on head, the expensive course in
    grooming.

He has bought books for me, afterwards praising
My book-taught erudition;
His refusal to face my fact makes me sacrosanct,
Would make him describe as modesty this confession.

Yet the view from this pedestal is pleasantly heady;
And perhaps, such is my elevation, he need never see
The imperfections which I certainly share
With the old loves, unloved now, who went before me.

Thus may I give to him the one great excellence
I have: my love for him, which alone he fails to praise.
If so, so be it. Let there be this sweet
Misunderstanding to the end of our shared days,

For above all am I glad to be his chosen,
And to be loved, albeit for the wrong reason.

Eric Millward

The Romantic Age

This one is entering her teens,
Ripe for sentimental scenes,
Has picked a gangling unripe male,
Sees herself in bridal veil,
Presses lips and tosses head,
Declares she's not too young to wed,
Informs you pertly you forget
Romeo and Juliet.
Do not argue, do not shout
Remind her how that one turned out.

Ogden Nash

Juliet

Sweet, good night!
This bud of love, by summer's ripening breath,
May prove a beauteous flower when next we meet.
Good night, good night! As sweet repose and rest
Come to thy heart as that within my breast.

My bounty is as boundless as the sea,
My love as deep, the more I give to thee
The more I have, for both are infinite.

William Shakespeare
(*from* Romeo and Juliet)

RIP

A girl in our village makes love in the churchyard.
She doesn't care who, but it must be the churchyard.
They say she prefers the old part to the new.
Green granite chippings, maybe,
Rankle. Worn slabs welcome.
And after, in her bedroom,
She sees the mirror's view
Of her shoulder embossed
In Loving Memory.

Ann, why do you do it, you've eight 'O' Levels?
Why not, Ann? If bones remember, you'll give
    them joy.
It's as good a place as any,
Close by nave, rood screen, chapel at ease,
Peal of the bells,
Bob Singles and Grandsire Doubles,
And when you half close your eyes,
The horned gargoyles choose.

But it has to happen.
Oh, Ann, tonight you were levelled.
William Jones, late of this parish,
Was cold beneath you, and his great-great-grandson
Warm above; and you rose,
Though your shoulder didn't know it,
In Glorious Expectation of the Life to Come.

Alan Garner

First Love

When you first combed back your fringe
Under the apple boughs
I thought you were like a flower
With the comb like a blossom at the front.

When you stretched out your white hand to me
To give me the apple
I felt for the first time the stir of love
Among the rose-red fruits of Autumn.

I breathed my love like a sigh
Upon your combed-back fringe.
I gave you my heart
Like a cup brimming with the wine of love.

The path lies empty before me now
Under the tree in the apple orchard,
When I asked: 'Who walked beside me along this
    narrow path?'
What I am missing is that first love.

Shimazaki Toson
(Translated by James Kirkup)

Years Ago

It was what we did not do that I remember,
Places with no markers left by us,
All of a summer, meeting every day,
A memorable summer of hot days,
Day after day of them, evening after evening.
Sometimes we would laze

Upon the river-bank, just touching hands
Or stroking one another's arms with grasses.
Swans floated by seeming to assert
Their dignity. But we too had our own
Decorum in the small-change of first love.

Nothing was elegiac or nostalgic,
We threw time in the river as we threw
Breadcrumbs to an inquisitive duck, and so
Day entered evening with a sweeping gesture,
Idly we talked of food and where to go.

This is the love that I knew long ago.
Before possession, passion, and betrayal.

Elizabeth Jennings

In Love

The Aeronaut to his Lady: a Sonnet

I
Through
Blue
Sky
Fly
To
You
Why?
Sweet
Love
Feet
Move
So
Slow.

Frank Sidgwick

I Like You

Although I saw you
The day before yesterday,
And yesterday and today,
This much is true –
I want to see you tomorrow, too!

Masuhito

I Love You Because

1 your hair falls in a cock's tail
2 your words are sweet and subtle
3 your dimples are big as coins
4 your teeth outshine pure jet grains*
5 your neck has an amulet
6 your hat has tassels on it
7 your ways are wise and witty
8 your mouth when you speak – oh boy!
9 your life is lived all alone
10 your eyes say things to a man.

Korean Folk Song
(Translated by Keith Bosley)

* *because they have been lacquered with a black cosmetic*

You're the top, you're the Coliseum
You're the top, you're the Louvre museum,
You're a melody from a symphony by Strauss,
You're a Bendel bonnet, a Shakespeare sonnet,
You're Mickey Mouse . . .

Cole Porter

The Man in the Opera Sings to His Loved One

You're like the jolliest picnic in a children's book,
like the bright sun in the morning is the way you
   look,
you're just the most beautiful dish that any cook could
   cook!

I simply adore kissing your ears and your toes,
it's all the course of true love – that's the way it goes –
you're wonderful enough to cancel out a whole week
   of woes!

I feel terribly happy that I'm the one you like,
my desires all run away with me like a racing bike,
I am amplified like the song that goes into the mike!

And all I can think about is: What did I ever do
to deserve the First Prize of a marvellous person like
   you?
Hooray! that Fate singled me out to be the head of
   the queue!

Gavin Ewart

Flowers you cultivate and prize,
But you're the fairest in my eyes!
Your merit sheds a rich perfume,
Which adds unto your native bloom.
'Tis you I wish to claim as mine
And take you for my Valentine.

To My Valentine

More than a catbird hates a cat,
Or a criminal hates a clue,
Or the Axis hates the United States,
That's how much I love you.

I love you more than a duck can swim,
And more than a grapefruit squirts,
I love you more than gin rummy is a bore,
And more than a toothache hurts.

As a shipwrecked sailor hates the sea,
Or a juggler hates a shove,
As a hostess detests unexpected guests,
That's how much you I love.

I love you more than a wasp can sting,
And more than the subway jerks,
I love you as much as a beggar needs a crutch,
And more than a hangnail irks.

I swear to you by the stars above,
And below, if such there be,
As the High Court loathes perjurious oaths,
That's how you're loved by me.

Ogden Nash

True Ways of Knowing

Not an ounce excessive, not an inch too little,
Our easy reciprocations. You let me know
The way a boat would feel, if it could feel,
The intimate support of water.

The news you bring me has been news forever,
So that I understand what a stone would say
If only a stone could speak. Is it sad a grassblade
Can't know how it is lovely?

Is it sad that you can't know, except by hearsay
(My gossiping failing words) that you are the way
A water is that can clench its palm and crumple
A boat's confiding timbers?

But that's excessive, and too little. Knowing
The way a circle would describe its roundness,
We touch two selves and feel, complete and gentle,
The intimate support of being.

The way that flight would feel a bird flying
(If it could feel) is the way a space that's in
A stone that's in a water would know itself
If it had our way of knowing.

Norman Macaig

The Confirmation

Yes, yours, my love, is the right human face.
I in my mind had waited for this long,
Seeing the false and searching for the true,
Then found you as a traveller finds a place
Of welcome suddenly amid the wrong
Valleys and rocks and twisting roads. But you,
What shall I call you? A fountain in a waste,
A well of water in a country dry,
Or anything that's honest and good, an eye
The makes the whole world bright. Your open heart,
Simple with giving, gives the primal deed,
The first good world, the blossom, the blowing seed,
The hearth, the steadfast land, the wandering sea,
Not beautiful or rare in every part,
But like yourself, as they were meant to be.

Edwin Muir

For Anne Gregory

'Never shall a young man,
Thrown into despair
By those great honey-coloured
Ramparts at your ear,
Love you for yourself alone
And not your yellow hair.'

'But I can get a hair-dye
And set such colour there,
Brown, or black, or carrot,
That young men in despair
May love me for myself alone
And not my yellow hair.'

'I heard an old religious man
But yesternight declare
That he had found a text to prove
That only God, my dear,
Could love you for yourself alone
And not your yellow hair.'

W. B. Yeats

Sonnet

If thou must love me, let it be for nought
Except for love's sake only. Do not say
'I love her for her smile – her look – her way
Of speaking gently – for a trick of thought
That falls in well with mine, and certes brought
A sense of pleasant ease on such a day –
For these things in themselves, Beloved, may
Be changed, or change for thee – and love, so
  wrought,
May be unwrought so. Neither love me for
Thine own dear pity's wiping my cheeks dry –
A creature might forget to weep, who bore
The comfort long, and lose thy love thereby!
But love me for love's sake, that evermore
Thou mayst love on, through love's eternity.

Elizabeth Barrett Browning

She

Have you seen but a bright lily grow,
   Before rude hands have touched it?
Ha' you marked but the fall o' the snow
   Before the soil hath smutched it?
Ha' you felt the wool o' the beaver,
   Or swansdown ever?
Or have smelt o' the bud o' the briar,
   Or the nard in the fire?
Or have tasted the bag of the bee?
O so white! O so soft! O so sweet is she!

Ben Jonson

Blackberry Sweet

Black girl   black girl
lips as curved as berries
full as grape bunches
sweet as blackberries

Black girl   black girl
when you walk you are
magic as a rising bird
or a falling star

Black girl   black girl
what's your spell to make
the heart in my breast
jump   stop   shake

Dudley Randall

To His Coy Mistress

Had we but world enough, and time,
This coyness, Lady, were no crime.
We would sit down, and think which way
To walk, and pass our long love's day.
Thou by the Indian Ganges' side
Shouldst rubies find: I by the tide
Of Humber would complain. I would
Love you ten years before the flood:
And you should, if you please, refuse
Till the conversion of the Jews.
My vegetable love should grow
Vaster than empires, and more slow.
An hundred years should go to praise
Thine eyes, and on thy forehead gaze.
Two hundred to adore each breast:
But thirty thousand to the rest.
An age at least to every part,
And the last age should show your heart;
For, Lady, you deserve this state;
Nor would I love at lower rate.

   But at my back I always hear
Time's wingèd chariot hurrying near:
And yonder all before us lie
Deserts of vast eternity.
Thy beauty shall no more be found;
Nor, in thy marble vault, shall sound

My echoing song: then worms shall try
That long-preserved virginity:
And your quaint honour turn to dust;
And into ashes all my lust.
The grave's a fine and private place,
But none, I think, do there embrace.
   Now, therefore, while the youthful glue
Sits on thy skin like morning dew,
And while thy willing soul transpires
At every pore with instant fires,
Now let us sport us while we may;
And now, like amorous birds of prey,
Rather at once our time devour,
Than languish in his slow-chapped power.
Let us roll all our strength, and all
Our sweetness, up into one ball:
And tear our pleasures with rough strife,
Thorough the iron grates of life.
Thus, though we cannot make our sun
Stand still, yet we will make him run.

Andrew Marvell

Message

Pick up the phone before it is too late
And dial my number. There's no time to spare —
Love is already turning into hate
And very soon I'll start to look elsewhere.

Good, old-fashioned men like you are rare —
You want to get to know me at a rate
That's guaranteed to drive me to despair.
Pick up the phone before it is too late.

Well, wouldn't it be nice to consummate
Our friendship while we've still got teeth and hair?
Just bear in mind that you are forty-eight
And dial my number. There's no time to spare.

Another kamikaze love affair?
No chance. This time I'll have to learn to wait
But one more day is more than I can bear —
Love is already turning into hate.

Of course, my friends say I exaggerate
And dramatize a lot. That may be fair
But it is no fun being in this state
And very soon I'll start to look elsewhere.

I know you like me but I wouldn't dare
Ring you again. Instead I'll concentrate
On sending thought-waves through the London air
And, if they reach you, please don't hesitate —
Pick up the phone.

Wendy Cope

Warning to Gloria

I wait for you whose half past six is seven
Or eight – or nine tomorrow: who may someday
Discover clocks as Christopher Columbus
Suddenly saw America. And, waiting,
I say to you who are not here, 'Remember,
I hate your large, magnificent indifference
To time because I love you: hate this waiting
To see and touch and hear you, to be near you.
And one day when you've kept me too long waiting
I may say something which you won't forgive me
Nor I forgive myself; and then, love, then what
Unthinkable ending? Try to think, remember
That love and hate are next-door neighbours meeting
Like day and night, like happiness and tears.'

A. S. J. Tessimond

Sonnet

Being your slave, what should I do but tend
Upon the hours and times of your desire?
I have no precious time at all to spend,
Nor services to do till you require.
Nor dare I chide the world-without-end hour
Whilst I, my sovereign, watch the clock for you,
Nor think the bitterness of absence sour
When you have bid your servant once adieu.
Nor dare I question with my jealous thought
Where you may be, or your affairs suppose,
But, like a sad slave, stay and think of naught
Save where you are how happy you make those.
  So true a fool is love that in your will,
    Though you do anything, he thinks no ill.

William Shakespeare

from Why Doesn't She Come?

Why doesn't she come?
  I know we said eight.
Or was it half-past?
That clock must be fast.
Why doesn't she come?
  She's ten minutes late.
I'll sit by the door
  And see her come in;
I've brought her a rose,
  I've borrowed a pin.
I'll be very severe,
I'll tell her, 'My dear,
You mustn't be late.'
It's a quarter past eight.
  Why doesn't she come?

Why doesn't she come?
   This must be the place.
She couldn't forget,
Or is she upset?
Why doesn't she come?
   Am I in disgrace?
Oh, well, if it's that,
We were both in the wrong –
I'll give her the rose
And say I was wrong.
I'll give her a kiss
And tell her I'm sorry –
'I'm *terribly* sorry . . .'
Why doesn't she come?

Perhaps she is ill –
I fancied last night
Her eyes were too bright –
   A feverish chill?
She's lying in bed,
She's light in the head!
She's dying – she's *dead!*
   Why doesn't she come?

Why doesn't she come?
Why doesn't she come?
It's nearly half-past.
Well, never again!
I'll send her the rose,
I won't say a word,
Just send her the rose –
She'd *laugh*, I suppose!
A flirt and a fraud!
I'll travel abroad,
I'll go to the East,
I'll shoot a wild beast.
And now for a drink,
I'll have a stiff drink –
A brandy, I think –
   And drown myself in it.
I'll shoot myself . . . Oh,
How I love her! – 'Hul-*lo!*
   What? *Late?* Not a minute!'

A. P. Herbert

Sonnet

How do I love thee? Let me count the ways.
I love thee to the depth and breadth and height
My soul can reach, when feeling out of sight
For the ends of Being and ideal Grace.
I love thee to the level of everyday's
Most quiet need, by sun and candle-light.
I love thee freely, as men strive for Right;
I love thee purely, as they turn from Praise.
I love thee with the passion put to use
In my old griefs, and with my childhood's faith.
I love thee with a love I seemed to lose
With my lost saints, – I love thee with the breath,
Smiles, tears, of all my life! – and, if God choose,
I shall but love thee better after death.

Elizabeth Barrett Browning

My True Love Hath My Heart, and I Have His

My true love hath my heart, and I have his,
  By just exchange one for the other given;
I hold his dear, and mine he cannot miss;
  There never was a better bargain driven.
His heart in me keeps me and him in one;
  My heart in him his thoughts and senses guides;
He loves my heart, for once it was his own;
  I cherish his, because in me it bides.
His heart his wound received from my sight;
  My heart was wounded with his wounded heart:
For as from me on him his hurt did light,
  So still me thought in me his hurt did smart.
    Both equal hurt, in this change sought one bliss:
    My true love hath my heart, and I have his.

Sir Philip Sidney

i carry your heart with me

i carry your heart with me (i carry it in
my heart) i am never without it (anywhere
i go you go, my dear; and whatever is done
by only me is your doing, my darling)
                                        i fear
no fate (for you are my fate, my sweet) i want
no world (for beautiful you are my world, my true)
and it's you are whatever a moon has always meant
and whatever a sun will always sing is you

here is the deepest secret nobody knows
(here is the root of the root and the bud of the bud
and the sky of the sky of a tree called life; which grows
higher than soul can hope or mind can hide)
and this is the wonder that's keeping the stars apart

i carry your heart (i carry it in my heart)

e e cummings

Skinscape

Your white skin and my brown skin
Make arcs and angles on the grey geometry
Of the sheet. Like white eggs and brown eggs
In maché sections, our grainy curves
Define the diagonals.
Your white egg shells and my brown egg shells
Are a study in the coolness of colour
And the precision of form,
A smooth and finished composition,
More true and more by accident
Than by design.

Susan Hamlyn

In Bloemfontein

Woman to man, they lie,
He not quite white
As she, nor she
So black as he.

Save where her stomach curves
His flesh and hers,
Commingling, match.
Eyes catch.

They dare not meet
Beyond the night,
Though their alternate
Thighs, locked tight,

Defy you to discriminate
Between his skin and hers.
To him Pass Laws
Apply; she knows no night.

But that pale strip her loins
Keep from the sun
Marks her, his tiger-woman,
White, while he's all one.

That strip convicts. He covers
With his hand the site
Of crime. Soon shutters,
Striping him with light

Peel colour from his hips –
She his woman, he
Her man, simply human
Like the heart beneath her lips.

A matter of degree
Elsewhere, no more;
But here, in Bloemfontein,
Keep closed the door.

Alan Ross

Gourmet

I would rather eat fish and chips
In the street with you
Than dine with everyone else in the whole
Wide world at the Ritz.

Anthony Astbury

The Little Language

When I am near you, I'm like a child,
I am still and simple, I am undefiled.
I speak my love in a forgotten tongue,
And use the words I knew when I was young.
My Love! You have restored me in a hundred ways,
You gave me back my happy childish days.

Anna Wickham

Love Me

Love me
but do not come too near
leave room for love
to laugh at its happiness
always let some of my blond hair
be free

Marian Wine
(Translated from Swedish by
Nadia Christensen)

Alisoun

From middle March to April
  When the spray begins to spring
The little birds of the air desire
  In their own tongue to sing.
While I, I live in longing
For the bliss that she may bring,
The loveliest living thing;
  To serve her is a boon.
A gracious chance for me was meant;
I know from heaven it was sent
That, from all women, my love was lent
  And left with Alisoun.

Fair is her hair and soft enough:
  Her eyes are black, her brow is chaste;
Her voice is light and laughs with love;
  Slight is her figure, small her waist.
Unless she comes or bids me wait
To take her as my own true mate,
I will not live, but, desperate,
  I'm like to perish soon.
A gracious chance for me was meant;
I know from heaven it was sent
That, from all women, my love was lent
  And left with Alisoun.

All night long I toss and wake;
   For thee alone my cheeks grow wan.
Lady, it is for thy sweet sake
   My longing rages on.
In all the world the wisest man
Cannot describe her bounty's span;
Her neck is whiter than the swan –
   The fairest maid in town.
A gracious chance for me was meant;
I know from heaven it was sent
That, from all women, my love was lent
   And left with Alisoun.

Anon.

To Mistress Anne

Mistress Anne
I am your man,
As you may well espy.
If you will be
Content with me,
I am your man.

But if you will
Keep company still
With every knave that comes by,
Then you will be
Forsaken of me,
That am your man.

But if you fain,
I tell you plain,
That I presently shall die,
I will not such
As loves too much,
That am your man.

For if you can
Love every man
That can flatter and lie,
Then are ye
No match for me,
That am your man.

For I will not take
No such kind of mate
(May all full well it trie!),
But off will ye cast
At any blast,
That am your man.

John Skelton

Teach the Making of Summer

Dave. Dear Dave.
I could write a letter
of only *Dear Dave.*
My favourite words echo
and whiz me round the world and back.

Did I tell you that when
we talk on the phone I cover
my other ear
to keep your voice in
so that it goes all round my head
And sinks and drifts all about my body?

Dave. Dear Dave.
I write on big paper
to keep your eyes pouring hungrily
over my naked thoughts.

Did I tell you that
next day after seeing you, the volume
of my feelings gets so turned up
it scares me other fellows might touch them?

Did I tell you that thinking suddenly
of a certain person can make
me gasp or gulp or sigh or make
a whimsical moan of a sound
or just hold on to anything near?

Dave. Dear Dave.
Can we start up a school
to teach the making of summer?
You and me have so much!

Rain clouds are heavy today.
An aeroplane passed was like
a submarine overhead, when
in your eyes
is a smile
to meet kisses.

Dave. Dear Dave.
Now, other things may well get done.
I have prayed today.

James Berry

Words, for E

The sky is blue, or something. Anyway, it's there.
Your words are hands, stroking me, stroking the sky,
Blue sky, names, people. It's marvellous. I'm king,
And your words are a line of ships. The guns fire.
Blue sky, names, people. I take the salute.

You are beautiful, sometimes. Now.
I feel for words for you. The ship rising, falling,
The horizon, a line rising, falling, behind your hair.
Words rise, spray. I like to think of you as giving
Structure. A gentleness. A constancy.

Tom Leonard

I have often walked down this street before
But the pavement always stayed beneath my feet before
All at once am I, several storeys high,
Standing here on the street where you live . . .

A. J. Lerner

Celia Celia

When I am sad and weary
When I think all hope has gone
When I walk along High Holborn
I think of you with nothing on

Adrian Mitchell

from Carmina Burana

She stood in her scarlet gown,
If any one touched her
The gown rustled.
Eia.
She stood, her face like a rose,
Shining she stood
And her mouth was a flower.
Eia.
She stood by the branch of a tree,
And writ her love on a leaf.

12th and 13th century

Song

Did you see me walking by the Buick Repairs?
I was thinking of you
having a Coke in the heat it was your face
I saw on the movie magazine, no it was Fabian's
I was thinking of you
and down at the railroad tracks where the station
has mysteriously disappeared
I was thinking of you
as the bus pulled away in the twilight
I was thinking of you
and right now

Frank O'Hara

All Change

So, they have done it. And here they are,
on a train to Nowhere-They-Know,
acting down a decision of days ago –
knowing that however far

they travel, and however fast,
something keeps pace with them that will
(their secret fear) perhaps outlast
what they would wish to think of as eternal.

And she, particularly, cannot rid her mind
of the thought of her children's eyes
(which must have seen the note they were
    meant to find
widening in what is, at first, surprise.)

He has said little, tactfully behaving
as he believes a lover should behave –
yet sensing the irony: that they are leaving
what once was love for what they now call Love.

Eric Millward

Paradox

Let us for this love
commit no crime,
not destroy others,
be calm in time
and let our love assume
the varied shapes it finds,
in its own pace and moments.

Let's have no hiddenness,
no deceitful trysts,
for others wait upon
our promised lives:

We can love more, unmarred,
if we resist;
and yet, my darling,
I am unconvinced.

Tom McGrath

Waiting

My love will come
will fling open her arms and fold me in them,
will understand my fears, observe my changes.
In from the pouring dark, from the pitch night
without stopping to bang the taxi door
she'll run upstairs through the decaying porch
burning with love and love's happiness,
She'll run dripping upstairs, she won't knock,
will take my head in her hands,
and when she drops her overcoat in a chair,
it will slide to the floor in a blue heap.

Yevgeny Yevtushenko

Alicante

An orange on the table
Your dress on the rug
And you in my bed
Sweet present of the present
Cool of night
Warmth of my life.

Jacques Prevert
(Translated by Lawrence Ferlinghetti)

Western wind, when wilt though blow
The small rain down can rain?
Christ, if my love were in my arms
And I in my bed again!

Anon.

Although I conquer All the Earth

Although I conquer all the earth,
Yet for me there is only one city.
In that city there is for me only one house;
And in that house, one room only;
And in that room, a bed.
And one woman sleeps there,
The shining joy and jewel of all my kingdom.

Ancient India

Strawberries

There were never strawberries
like the ones we had
that sultry afternoon
sitting on the step
of the open french window
facing each other
your knees held in mine
the blue plates in our laps
the strawberries glistening
in the hot sunlight
we dipped them in sugar
looking at each other
not hurrying the feast
for one to come
the empty plates
laid on the stone together
with the two forks crossed
and I bent towards you
sweet in that air
in my arms
abandoned like a child

from your eager mouth
the taste of strawberries
in my memory
lean back again
let me love you
let the sun beat
on our forgetfulness
one hour of all
the heat intense
and summer lightning
on the Kilpatrick hills
let the storm wash the plates

Edwin Morgan

Renouncement

I must not think of thee; and, tired yet strong,
  I shun the thought that lurks in all delight –
The thought of thee – and in the blue Heaven's
  height,
And in the sweetest passage of a song.
Oh, just beyond the fairest thoughts that throng
This breast, the thought of thee waits hidden yet
  bright;
  But it must never, never come in sight;
I must stop short of thee the whole day long.

But when sleep comes to close each difficult day,
  When night gives pause to the long watch I keep,
    And all my bonds I needs must loose apart,
Must doff my will as raiment laid away, –
  With the first dream that comes with the first sleep
    I run, I run, I am gathered to thy heart.

Alice Meynell

Colours

When your face
appeared over my crumpled life
at first I understood
only the poverty of what I have.
Then its particular light
on woods, on rivers, on the sea,
became my beginning in the coloured world
in which I had not yet had my beginning.
I am so frightened, I am so frightened,
of the unexpected sunrise finishing,
of revelations
and tears and the excitement finishing.
I don't fight it, my love is this fear,
I nourish it who can nourish nothing,
love's slipshod watchman.
Fear hems me in.
I am conscious that these minutes are short
and that the colours in my eyes will vanish
when your face sets.

Yevgeny Yevtushenko

The Hill

Breathless, we flung us on the windy hill,
  Laughed in the sun, and kissed the lovely grass.
  You said, 'Through glory and ecstasy we pass;
Wind, sun, and earth remain, the birds sing still,
When we are old, are old . . .' 'And when we die
  All's over that is ours; and life burns on
Through other lovers, other lips,' said I,
  'Heart of my heart, our heaven is now, is won!'

'We are Earth's best, that learnt her lesson here.
  Life is our cry. We kept the faith!' we said;
  'We shall go down with unreluctant tread
Rose-crowned into the darkness!' . . . Proud we were,
  And laughed, that had such brave true things to say
  – And then you suddenly cried, and turned away.

Rupert Brooke

Winter Love

Let us have winter loving that the heart
May be in peace and ready to partake
Of the slow pleasure spring would wish to hurry
Or that in summer harshly would awake,
And let us fall apart, O gladly weary,
The white skin shaken like a white snowflake.

Elizabeth Jennings

She Tells Her Love While Half Asleep

She tells her love while half asleep
    In the dark hours,
        With half-words whispered low:
As Earth stirs in her winter sleep
    And puts out grass and flowers
        Despite the snow,
        Despite the falling snow.

Robert Graves

Love Comes Quietly

Love comes quietly,
finally, drops
about me, on me,
in the old ways.

What did I know
thinking myself
able to go
alone all the way.

Robert Creeley

Sonnet

If there be any one can take my place
And make you happy whom I grieve to grieve,
Think not that I can grudge it, but believe
I do commend you to that nobler grace,
That readier wit than mine, that sweeter face;
Yea, since your riches make me rich, conceive
I too am crowned, while bridal crowns I weave,
And thread the bridal dance with jocund pace.
For if I did not love you, it might be
That I should grudge you some one dear delight;
But since the heart is yours that was mine own.
Your pleasure is my pleasure, right my right,
Your honourable freedom makes me free,
And you companioned I am not alone.

Christina Rossetti

Sonnet

it may not always be so; and i say
that if your lips, which i have loved should touch
another's, and your dear strong fingers clutch
his heart, as mine in time not far away;
if on another's face your sweet hair lay
in such a silence as i know, or such
great writhing words as, uttering overmuch,
stand helplessly before the spirit at bay;

if this should be, i say if this should be –
you of my heart, send me a little word;
that i may go unto him, and take his hands,
saying, Accept all happiness from me.
Then shall i turn my face, and hear one bird
sing terribly afar in the lost lands.

e e cummings

The Good Morrow

I wondered by my troth, what thou, and I
　　Did, till we loved? were we not weaned till then,
But sucked on country pleasures, childishly?
　　Or snorted we in the seven sleepers' den?
'Twas so; but this, all pleasures fancies be.
If ever any beauty I did see,
Which I desired, and got, 'twas but a dream of thee.

And now good morrow to our waking souls,
　　Which watch not one another out of fear;
For love, all love of other sights controls,
　　And makes one little room, an every where.
Let sea-discoverers to new worlds have gone,
Let maps to others, worlds on worlds have shown,
　　Let us possess one world, each hath one, and is one.

My face in thine eye, thine in mine appears,
　　And true plain hearts do in the faces rest,
Where can we find two better hemispheres
　　Without sharp north, without declining west?
What ever dies, was not mixed equally;
If our two loves be one, or, thou and I
Love so alike, that none do slacken, none can die.

John Donne

LOVE TOKENS

A blade of grass

You ask for a poem.
I offer you a blade of grass.
You say it is not good enough.
You ask for a poem.

I say this blade of grass will do.
It has dressed itself in frost,
It is more immediate
Than any image of my making.

You say it is not a poem,
It is a blade of grass and grass
Is not quite good enough.
I offer you a blade of grass.

You are indignant.
You say it is too easy to offer grass.
It is absurd.
Anyone can offer a blade of grass.

You ask for a poem
And so I wrote you a tragedy about
How a blade of grass
Becomes more and more difficult to offer.

And about how as you grow older
A blade of grass
Becomes more difficult to accept.

Brian Patten

If you love me, love me true,
Send me a ribbon and let it be blue.
If you hate me let it be seen
Send me a ribbon and let it be green.

I Will Make You Brooches

I will make you brooches and toys for your delight
Of bird-song at morning and star-shine at night.
I will make a palace fit for you and me
Of green days in forests and blue days at sea.

I will make my kitchen, and you shall keep your room,
Where white flows the river and bright blows the
    broom,
And you shall wash your linen and keep your body
    white
In rainfall at morning and dewfall at night.

And this shall be for music when no one else is near,
The fine song for singing, the rare song to hear!
That only I remember, that only you admire,
Of the broad road that stretches and the roadside fire.

Robert Louis Stevenson

The Glow-Worm

Among all lovely things my Love had been;
Had noted well the stars, all flowers that grew
About her home; but she had never seen
A glow-worm, never one, and this I knew.

While riding near her home one stormy night
A single glow-worm did I chance to espy;
I gave a fervent welcome to the sight,
And from my horse I leapt; great joy had I.

Upon a leaf the glow-worm did I lay,
To bear it with me through the stormy night:
And, as before, it shone without dismay;
Albeit putting forth a fainter light.

When to the dwelling of my Love I came,
I went into the orchard quietly;
And left the glow-worm, blessing it by name,
Laid safely by itself, beneath a tree.

The whole next day, I hoped, and hoped with fear;
At night the glow-worm shone beneath the tree;
I led my Lucy to the spot, 'Look here,'
Oh! joy it was for her, and joy for me!

William Wordsworth

Girl, Boy, Flower, Bicycle

This girl
Waits at the corner for
This Boy
Freewheeling on his bicycle.
She holds
A flower in her hand
A gold flower
In her hands she holds
The sun.
With power between his thighs
The boy
Comes smiling to her
He rides
A bicycle that glitters like
The wind.
This boy this girl
They walk
In step with the wind
Arm in arm
They climb the level street

To where
Laid on the glittering handlebars
The flower
Is round and shining as
The sun.

M. K. Joseph

Ballad

It was not in the Winter
    Our loving lot was cast;
It was the Time of Roses, –
    We pluck'd them as we pass'd;

That churlish season never frown'd
    On early lovers yet: –
Oh, no – the world was newly crown'd
    With flowers when first we met!

'Twas twilight, and I bade you go,
    But still you held me fast;
It was the Time of Roses, –
    We pluck'd them as we pass'd. –

What else could peer thy glowing cheek.
    That tears began to stud!
And when I ask'd the like of Love,
    You snatched a damask bud;

And oped it to the dainty core,
    Still glowing to the last, –
It was the Time of Roses, –
    We pluck'd them as we pass'd!

Thomas Hood

Go, Lovely Rose

Go, lovely rose,
  Tell her that wastes her time and me,
That now she knows,
  When I resemble her to thee
  How sweet and fair she seems to be.

Tell her that's young,
  And shuns to have her graces spied,
That hadst thou sprung
  In deserts where no men abide,
  Thou must have uncommended died.

Small is the worth
  Of beauty from the light retired:
Bid her come forth,
  Suffer herself to be desired,
  And not blush so to be admired.

Then die – that she
  The common fate of all things rare
May read in thee;
  How small a part of time they share
  That are so wondrous sweet and fair!

Edmund Waller

Roses are red, my love
Violets are blue
Sugar is sweet, my love
But not so sweet as you.

Sonnet

Beloved, thou hast brought me many flowers
Plucked in the garden, all the summer through
And winter, and it seemed as if they grew
In this close room, nor missed the sun and
    showers,
So, in the like name of that love of ours,
Take back these thoughts which here unfolded
    too,
And which on warm and cold days I withdrew
From my heart's ground. Indeed, those beds and
    bowers
Be overgrown with bitter weeds and rue,
And wait thy weeding; yet here's eglantine,
Here's ivy! – take them, as I used to do
Thy flowers, and keep them where they shall
    not pine.
Instruct thine eyes to keep their colours true,
And tell thy soul, their roots are left in mine.

Elizabeth Barrett Browning

One Perfect Rose

A single flow'r he sent me, since we met.
  All tenderly his messenger he chose;
Deep-hearted, pure, with scented dew still wet –
  One perfect rose.

I knew the language of the floweret;
  'My fragile leaves,' it said, 'his heart enclose.'
Love long has taken for his amulet
  One perfect rose.

Why is it no one ever sent me yet
  One perfect limousine, do you suppose?
Ah no, it's always just my luck to get
  One perfect rose.

Dorothy Parker

I Won't Send Roses

I won't send roses or hold the door
I won't remember which dress you wore
My heart is too much in control
The lack of romance in my soul
Will turn you grey, dear
So stay away, dear
Forget my shoulder
When you're in need
Forgetting birthdays
Is guaranteed
And should I love you
You would be the last to know
I won't send roses –
And roses suit you so.

Jerry Herman

My love is like a cabbage
  Divided into two,
The leaves I give to others,
  But the heart I give to you!

O My Luve's Like a Red, Red Rose

O my Luve's like a red, red rose
   That's newly sprung in June:
O my Luve's like the melodie
  That's sweetly play'd in tune.

As fair art thou, my bonnie lass,
  So deep in luve am I:
And I will luve thee still, my dear,
  Till a' the seas gang dry:

Till a' the seas gang dry, my dear,
  And the rocks melt wi' the sun;
I will luve thee still, my dear,
  While the sands o' life shall run.

And fare thee weel, my only Luve!
  And fare thee weel a while!
And I will come again, my Luve,
  Tho' it were ten thousand mile.

Robert Burns

And Kisses

Come hither, womankind and all their worth,
Give me thy kisses as I call them forth.
Give me the billing kiss, that of the dove,
    A kiss of love;
The melting kiss, a kiss that doth consume
    To a perfume;
The extract kiss, of every sweet a part,
    A kiss of art;
The kiss which ever stirs some new delight,
    A kiss of might;
The twaching smacking kiss, and when you cease,
    A kiss of peace;
The music kiss, crochet-and-quaver time;
    The kiss of rhyme;
The kiss of eloquence, which doth belong
    Unto the tongue;
The kiss of all the sciences in one,
    The Kiss alone.
So, 'tis enough.

Edward, Lord Herbert of Cherbury

A Kiss

O, that joy so soon should waste!
  Or so sweet a bliss
    As a kiss,
Might not forever last!
So sugared, so melting, so soft, so delicious,
  The dew that lies on roses,
  When the morn herself discloses,
    Is not so precious.
O, rather than I would it smother,
Were I to taste such another;
  It should be my wishing
  That I might die kissing.

Ben Jonson

Sonnet

First time he kissed me, he but only kissed
The fingers of this hand wherewith I write,
And ever since, it grew more clean and white,
Slow to world-greetings, quick with its 'Oh, list,'
When the angels speak. A ring of amethyst
I could not wear here, plainer to my sight,
Than that first kiss. The second passed in height
The first, and sought the forehead, and half missed,
Half falling on the hair. O beyond meed!
That was the chrism of love, which love's own crown,
With sanctifying sweetness, did precede.
The third upon my lips was folded down
In perfect purple state; since when, indeed,
I have been proud and said, 'My love, my own.'

Elizabeth Barrett Browning

The Kiss

'I saw you take his kiss!' ''Tis true.'
'O, modesty!' ''Twas strictly kept:
He thought me asleep; at least I knew
He thought I thought he thought I slept.'

Coventry Patmore

To Electra

I dare not ask a kisse;
   I dare not beg a smile;
Lest having that, or this,
   I might grow proud the while.

No, no, the utmost share
   Of my desire, shall be
Onely to kisse that Aire,
   That lately kissed thee.

Robert Herrick

Jenny Kiss'd Me

Jenny kiss'd me when we met,
  Jumping from the chair she sat in;
Time, you thief, who love to get
  Sweets into your list, put that in!
Say I'm weary, say I'm sad,
  Say that health and wealth have missed me,
Say I'm growing old, but add,
  Jenny kiss'd me.

Leigh Hunt

Jenny kiss'd me when we met,
  Jumping from the chair she sat
    in;
Time, you thief, who love to get
  Sweets into your lists, put that
    in!
Say I'm weary, say I'm old,
  Say that health and wealth have
    missed me,
Say I've had a filthy cold
  Since Jenny kiss'd me.

Paul Dehn

Jenny kiss'd me in a dream;
  So did Elsie, Lucy, Cora,
Bessie, Gwendolyn, Eupheme,
  Alice, Adelaide and Dora.
Say of honor I'm devoid.
  Say monogamy has miss'd me,
But don't say to Dr Freud
  Jenny kiss'd me.

Franklin P. Adams

The Kiss

Give me, my love, that billing kiss
   I taught you one delicious night,
When, turning epicures in bliss,
   We tried inventions of delight.

Come, gently steal my lips along,
   And let your lips in murmurs move, –
Ah, no! – again – that kiss was wrong –
How can you be so dull, my love?

'Cease, cease!' the blushing girl replied –
   And in her milky arms she caught me –
'How can you thus your pupil chide;
   You know *'twas in the dark* you taught me!'

Thomas Moore

The Look

Strephon kissed me in the spring
   Robin in the fall,
But Colin only looked at me
   And never kissed at all.

Strephon's kiss was lost in jest,
   Robin's lost in play,
But the kiss in Colin's eyes
   Haunts me night and day.

Sara Teasdale

Gifts of Love

I gave them to you
for your earlobes, your fingers. I gilded
the time on your wrist,
I hunt lots of glittery things on you
so you'd sway for me in the wind, so you'd
chime softly over me
to soothe my sleep.

I comforted you with apples, as it says
in the Song of Songs,
I lined your bed with them,
so we could roll smoothly on red apple-bearings.

I covered your skin with a pink chiffon,
transparent as baby lizards – the ones with
black diamond eyes on summer nights.

You helped me to live for a couple of months
without needing religion
or a point of view.

You gave me a letter opener made of silver.
Real letters aren't opened that way;
they're torn open,
torn, *torn*.

Yehuda Amichai
(Translated by Chana Bloch and Stephen Mitchell)

The Letter's Triumph

(A Fancy)

Yes: I perceive it's to your Love
You are bent on sending me. That this is so
    Your words and phrases prove!

And now I am folded, and start to go,
Where you, my writer, have no leave to come:
    My entry none will know!

And I shall catch her eye, and dumb
She'll keep, should my unnoised arrival be
    Hoped for, or troublesome.

My face she'll notice readily:
And, whether she care to meet you, or care not,
    She will perforce meet me;

Take me to closet or garden-plot
And, blushing or pouting, bend her eyes quite near,
    Moved much, or never a jot.

And while you wait in hope and fear,
Far from her cheeks and lips, snug I shall stay
    In close communion there,

    And hear her heart-beats, things you may say,
As near her naked fingers, sleeve, or glove
    I lie – ha-ha! – all day.

Thomas Hardy

The Letter

I take my pen in hand

                    there was a meadow
beside a field of oats, beside a wood,
beside a road, beside a day spread out
green at the edges, yellow at the heart.
The dust lifted a little, a finger's breadth;
the word of the wood pigeon travelled slow,
a slow half-pace behind the tick of time.

To tell you I am well and thinking of you

and of the walk through the meadow, and of another
    walk
along the neat piled ruin of the town
under a pale heaven empty of all but death
and rain beginning. The river ran beside.

It has been a long time since I wrote. I have no news.

I put my head between my hands and hope
my heart will choke me. I put out my hand
to touch you and touch air. I turn to sleep
and find a nightmare, hollowness and fear.

And by the way, I have had no letter now
For eight weeks, it must be

a long eight weeks,
because you have nothing to say, nothing at all,
not even to record your emptiness
or guess what's to become of you, without love.

I know that you have cares,

ashes to shovel, broken glass to mend
and many a cloth to patch before the sunset.

Write to me soon and tell me how you are.

if you still tremble, sweat and glower, still stretch
a hand for me at dusk, play me the tune,
show me the leaves and towers, the lamb, the rose.

Because I always wish to hear of you

and feel my heart swell and the blood run out
at the ungraceful syllable of your name
said through the scent of stocks, the little snore of fire,
the shoreless waves of symphony, the murmuring night.

I will end this letter now. I am yours with love.

Always with love, with love.

Elizabeth Riddell

This is to Let You Know

This is to let you know
That there was no moon last night
And that the tide was high
And that on the broken horizon glimmered the lights
  of ships
Twenty at least, like a sedate procession passing by.

This is to let you know
That when I'd turned out the lamp
And in the dark I lay
That suddenly piercing loneliness, like a knife,
Twisted my heart, for you were such a long long way
  away.

This to let you know
That there are no English words
That ever could explain
How, quite without warning, lovingly you were here
Holding me close, smoothing away the idiotic pain.

This is to let you know
That all that I feel for you
Can never wholly go.
I love you and miss you, even two hours away,
With all my heart. This is to let you know.

Noel Coward

Welsh Love Letter

Were all the peaks of Gwynedd
In one huge mountain piled,
Cnicht on Moelwyn,
Moel-y-gest, Moel Hebog,
And Eryri on top,
And all between us,
I'd climb them climb them
All!
To reach you.
O, how I love you!

Were all the streams of Gwynedd
In one great river joined,
Dwyfor, Dwyryd,
Glaslyn, Ogwen,
And Mawddach in flood,
And all between us,
I'd swim them swim them
All!
To reach you.
O, how I love you!

Were all the forts of Gwynedd
In one great fortress linked,
Caer and castle,
Cricieth, Harlech,
Conwy, Caernarfon,
And all in flames,
I'd jump them jump them
All!
To reach you.
O, how I love you!

See you Saturday,
If it's not raining.

Michael Burn

The 'Darling' Letters

Some keep them in shoeboxes away from the light,
sore memories blinking out as the lid lifts,
their own recklessness written all over them.
   My own . . .
Private jokes, no longer comprehended, pull their
   punchlines,
fall flat in the gaps between endearments. *What
are you wearing?*

                    Don't ever change.
They start with *Darling;* end in recriminations,
absence, sense of loss. Even now, the fist's bud flowers
into trembling, the fingers trace each line and see
the future then. *Always . . .* Nobody burns them,
the *Darling* letters, stiff in their cardboard coffins.

Babykins . . . We all had strange names
which make us blush, as though we'd murdered
someone under an alias, long ago. *I'll die
without you. Die.* Once in a while, alone,
we take them out to read again, the heart thudding
like a spade on buried bones.

Carol Ann Duffy

LoVe and Marriage

Prayer to St Catherine*

St Catherine, St Catherine, O lend me thine aid,
And grant that I never may die an old maid.

A husband, St Catherine,
A *good* one, St Catherine;
But arn-a-one better than
Narn-a-one, St Catherine.

Sweet St Catherine,
A husband, St Catherine,
Handsome, St Catherine,
Rich, St Catherine.
Soon, St Catherine!

Anon.

*St Catherine is the patron saint of spinsters

*If one day you would be wed,
Turn your bed from foot to head.*

'Come, come,' said Tom's father, 'at your time
   of life,
There's no longer excuse for thus playing the
   rake –
It is time, you should think, boy, of taking a
   wife.'
'Why so it is, father, pray whose shall I take?'

Thomas Moore

Love and marriage, love and marriage
Go together like a horse and carriage
Dad was told by mother
You can't have one, you can't have none, you
   can't have one without the other.

S. Cahn

Bide Awhile

I am my mammy's ae bairn,
　　Wi' unco[1] folk I weary, sir;
And lying in a man's bed,
　　I'm fleyed wad mak' me eerie, sir.

I'm o'er young to marry yet;
　　I'm o'er young to marry yet;
I'm o'er young – 'twad be a sin
　　To tak' me frae my mammy yet.

My mammy coft[2] me a new gown,
　　The kirk maun ha'e the gracing o't;
Were I to lie wi' you, kind sir,
　　I'm feared ye'd spoil the lacing o't.

Hallowmas is come and gane,
　　The nights are lang in winter, sir;
An' you an' I in ae bed
　　In trouth I dare na venture, sir.

[1] strange
[2] bought

Fu' loud and shrill the frosty wind
　　Blaws through the leafless timmer, sir;
But if ye come this gate again,
　　I'll aulder be gin summer, sir.

I'm o'er young to marry yet;
　　I'm o'er young to marry yet;
I'm o'er young – 'twad be a sin
　　To tak' me frae my mammy yet.

Robert Burns

To Know Whom One Shall Marry
(Speak While Knitting a Garter)

This knot I knit,
To know the thing, I know not yet,
That I may see,
The man that shall my husband be,
How he goes, and what he wears,
And what he does, all days, and years.

John Aubrey

from Waiting at the church

I'm in a nice bit of trouble, I confess;
   Somebody with me has had a game.
I should by now be a proud and happy bride,
   But I've still got to keep my single name.
I was proposed to by Obadiah Binks
   In a very gentlemanly way;
Lent him all my money so that he could buy a home,
   And punctually at twelve o'clock today –

There was I, waiting at the church, waiting at the
      church, waiting at the church –
   When I found he'd left me in the lurch,
   Lor, how it did upset me!
All at once he sent me round a note,
   Here's the very note,
   This is what he wrote –
'Can't get away to marry you today,
   My wife won't let me!'

Fred W. Leigh

Responsibility

'Tis easy enough to be twenty-one:
'Tis easy enough to marry;
But when you try both games at once
'Tis a bloody big load to carry.

Anon.

Susan Simpson

Sudden swallows swiftly skimming,
   Sunset's slowly spreading shade,
Silvery songsters sweetly singing
   Summer's soothing serenade.

Susan Simpson strolled sedately,
   Stifling sobs, suppressing sighs.
Seeing Stephen Slocum, stately
   She stopped, showing some surprise.

'Say,' said Stephen, 'sweetest sigher;
   Say, shall Stephen spouseless stay?'
Susan, seeming somewhat shyer,
   Showed submissiveness straightway.

Summer's season slowly stretches,
   Susan Simpson Slocum she –
So she signed some simple sketches –
   Soul sought soul successfully.

Six Septembers Susan swelters;
   Six sharp seasons snow supplied;
Susan's satin sofa shelters
   Six small Slocums side by side.

Anon.

A Scottish Proverb

He's a fool that marries at Yule,
For when the corn's to shear the bairn's to bear.

Anon.

I'm getting married in the morning
Ding dong the bells begin to chime
Pull out the stopper
Let's have a whopper –
But get me to the church on time.

A. J. Lerner

Propitious Days for Weddings

Monday for wealth,
Tuesday for health,
Wednesday the best day of all;
Thursday for crosses,
Friday for losses,
Saturday no luck at all.

Anon.

On Ladies' Accomplishments

Your dressing, dancing, gadding, where's the good in?
Sweet lady, tell me – can you make a pudding?

Anon.

Surnames to be Avoided in Marriage

To change the name, and not the letter,
Is a change for the worse, and not for the better.

Anon.

Epithalamion

Singing, today I married my white girl
beautiful in a barley field.
Green on thy finger a grass blade curled,
so with this ring I thee wed, I thee wed,
and send our love to the loveless world
of all the living and all the dead.

Now, no more than vulnerable human,
we, more than one, less than two,
are nearly ourselves in a barley field –
and only love is the rent that's due
though the bailiffs of time return anew
to all the living but not the dead.

Shipwrecked, the sun sinks down harbours
of a sky, unloads its liquid cargoes
of marigolds, and I and my white girl
lie still in the barley – who else wishes
to speak, what more can be said
by all the living against all the dead?

Come then all you wedding guests:
green ghost of trees, gold of barley,
you blackbird priests in the field,
you wind that shakes the pansy head
fluttering on a stalk like a butterfly;
come the living and come the dead.

Listen flowers, birds, winds, worlds,
tell all today that I married
more than a white girl in the barley –
for today I took to my human bed
flower and bird and wind and world,
and all the living and all the dead.

Dannie Abse

The Marriage of True Minds

Let me not to the marriage of true minds
Admit impediments. Love is not love
Which alters when it alteration finds,
Or bends with the remover to remove:
O, no! it is an ever-fixèd mark,
That looks on tempests and is never shaken;
It is the star to every wandering bark,
Whose worth's unknown, although his height
     be taken.
Love's not Time's fool, though rosy lips and
     cheeks
Within his bending sickle's compass come;
Love alters not with his brief hours and weeks,
But bears it out even to the edge of doom.
If this be error, and upon me prov'd,
I never writ, nor no man ever lov'd.

William Shakespeare

A Slice of Wedding Cake

Why have such scores of lovely, gifted girls
   Married impossible men?
Simple self-sacrifice may be ruled out,
   And missionary endeavour, nine times out of ten.

Repeat 'impossible men': not merely rustic,
   Foul-tempered or depraved
(Dramatic foils chosen to show the world
   How well women behave, and always have behaved).

Impossible men: idle, illiterate,
   Self-pitying, dirty, sly,
For whose appearance even in City parks
   Excuses must be made to casual passers-by.

Has God's supply of tolerable husbands
   Fallen, in fact, so low?
Or do I always over-value woman
   At the expense of man?
                Do I?
                    It might be so.

Robert Graves

Some starry night when her kisses make you tingle
She'll hold you tight and you'll hate yourself for being
  single
And all at once it seems so nice
The folks are throwing shoes and rice
You hurry to a spot
That's just a dot
On the map
And then –
You wonder how it all came about
It's too late now there's no getting out
You fell in love
And love is –
THE TENDER TRAP

S. Cahn

On My Wedding-Day

Here's a happy new year! but with reason
  I beg you'll permit me to say –
Wish me *many* returns of the *season*,
  But as *few* as you please of the day.

Lord Byron

this little bride & groom

this little bride & groom are
standing) in a kind
of crown he dressed
in black candy she

veiled with candy white
carrying a bouquet of
pretend flowers this
candy crown with this candy

little bride & little
groom in it kind of stands on
a thin ring which stands on a much
less thin very much more

big & kinder of ring & which
kinder of stands on a
much more than very much
biggest & thickest & kindest

of ring & all one two three rings
are cake & everything is protected by
cellophane against anything (because
nothing really exists

e e cummings

Take My Plastic Flowers

Take my plastic flowers
and my duplicated love-letters
with adjectives chosen by admen.
Take my marshmallow heart
and say yes.
Then we can go
and have a cassette tape join us
in everlasting wedlock to the building society.
Put on your best clothes
and your freshest smile
let's pretend to be people.

Bjorn Nilsen
(Translated by Penny English and Eric Barber)

Some wed for gold and some for pleasure,
And some wed only at their leisure,
But if you wish to wait and weep,
When e'er you wed,
  look well before you leap.

The wedding day appointed was
  And wedding clothes provided,
But ere that day did come, alas!
  He sickened and he dieded.

Bideford Churchyard, Devon

Why Am I Always the Bridesmaid?

Why am I dressed in these beautiful clothes?
   What is the matter with me?
I've been the bridesmaid for twenty-two brides;
   This time'll make twenty-three.
Twenty-two ladies I've helped off the shelf;
   No doubt it seems a bit strange:
Being the bridesmaid is no good to me;
   And I think I could do with a change.

Chorus

Why am I always the bridesmaid?
   Never the blushing bride?
      Ding-dong! wedding bells
      Only ring for other gels;
But some find day –
   Oh, let it be soon! –
I shall wake up in the morning
   On my own honeymoon.

Charles Collins and Fred W. Leigh

The Bridesmaid

O bridesmaid, ere the happy knot was tied,
Thine eyes so wept that they could hardly see;
Thy sister smiled and said, 'No tears for me!
A happy bridesmaid makes a happy bride.'
And then, the couple standing side by side,
Love lighted down between them full of glee,
And over his left shoulder laugh'd at thee,
'O happy bridesmaid, make a happy bride.'
And all at once a pleasant truth I learn'd,
For while the tender service made thee weep,
I loved thee for the tear thou couldst not hide,
And prest thy hand, and knew the press return'd,
And thought, 'My life is sick of single sleep:
O happy bridesmaid, make a happy bride!'

Alfred, Lord Tennyson

Les Sylphides

Life in a day: he took his girl to the ballet:
Being short-sighted himself could hardly see it –
    The white skirts in the grey
    Glade and the swell of the music
    Lifting the white sails.

Calyx upon calyx, canterbury bells in the breeze
The flowers on the left mirror to the flowers on the
  right
    And the naked arms above
    The powdered faces moving
    Like seaweed in a pool.

Now, he thought, we are floating – ageless, oarless –
Now there is no separation, from now on
    You will be wearing white
    Satin and a red sash
    Under the waltzing trees.

But the music stopped, the dancers took their curtain,
The river had come to a lock – a shuffle of
   programmes –
      And we cannot continue down-
      Stream unless we are ready
      To enter the lock and drop.

So they were married – to be the more together –
And found they were never again so much together,
      Divided by the morning tea,
      By the evening paper,
      By children and tradesmen's bills.

Waking at times in the night she found assurance
In his regular breathing but wondered whether
      It was really worth it and where
      The river had flowed away
      And where were the white flowers.

Louis MacNeice

The Honeymoon is Over

The honeymoon is over
And he has left for work
Whistling something obvious from La Bohème
And carrying a brown calfskin attaché case
I never dreamed he was capable of owning,
Having started the day
With ten pushups and a cold shower
Followed by a hearty breakfast.

(What do we actually have in common?)

The honeymoon is over
And I am dry-mopping the floor
In a green Dacron dry-mopping outfit from Saks,
Wondering why I'm not dancing in the dark,
Or rejecting princes,
Or hearing people gasp at my one-man show,
My god, so beautiful and so gifted!

(The trouble is I never knew a prince.)

The honeymoon is over
And we find that dining by candlelight makes us
   squint,
And that all the time
I was letting him borrow my comb and hang up his
   wet raincoat in my closet
I was really waiting
To stop letting him.
And that all the time
He was saying how he loved my chicken pot pie,
He was really waiting
To stop eating it.

(I guess they call this getting to know each other.)

Judith Viorst

Hardly Believable Horace and Hattie in Hell

Horace and Hattie, in cacophonous concert,
    Lived to a dual and discordant tune,
They could and they did disagree about everything
    Under the sun, and also the moon,
And if one said, 'Nice morning', the other infallibly
    Pronounced it a horrible afternoon,
And if either one triumphed in a point at issue
    (And no point was not) then the victory balloon
Would be savagely pierced when the narrowest opening
    For vengeance was glimpsed. They did not commune:
They spoke to each other to accuse, to exclude,
    To ensure and enrage, to impair and impugn.

Which makes it the stranger that they slept together
  Where even in the night like poisonous rain
Exchanged unpleasantries dripped in the darkness –
  Miss no chance where a particle of pain
Might yet be extracted was their changeless motto
  And no opportunity passed in vain –
So they sharpened themselves like knives on each other
  Where once more sweetly they had lain
When theirs was a house where love was living
  Whose ghost would not sleepwalk again,
Never a shadow, never a whisper,
  Not a whisker, not a grain.

So Hattie died, and she died with a rattle
  That threw the points in Horace's head
And his heart on its journey grated, slowed
  And turned like an engine in a turning-shed
And headed back down through the wailing tunnel
  Of the years, of the cold things done and said,
And he went by the land and he came by the water
  Of unshed tears on wounds unbled,
And he lay on his back in his clothes in the morning
  On that reconsecrated bed,
Floor of the ocean of a marriage, and cried
  Like the sea, 'My love, my love is dead!'

Kit Wright

One Flesh

Lying apart now, each in a separate bed,
He with a book, keeping the light on late,
She like a girl dreaming of childhood,
All men elsewhere – it is as if they wait
Some new event: the book he holds unread,
Her eyes fixed on the shadows overhead.

Tossed up like flotsam from a former passion,
How cool they lie. They hardly ever touch,
Or if they do it is like a confession
Of having little feeling – or too much.
Chastity faces them, a destination
For which their whole lives were a preparation.

Strangely apart, yet strangely close together,
Silence between them like a thread to hold
And not wind in. And time itself's a feather
Touching them gently. Do they know they're old,
These two who are my father and my mother
Whose fire from which I came, has now grown cold?

Elizabeth Jennings

On Giles and Joan

Who says that Giles and Joan at discord be?
The observing neighbours no such mood can see.
Indeed, poor Giles repents he married ever.
But that his Joan doth too. And Giles would never,
By his free will, be in Joan's company.
No more would Joan he should. Giles riseth early,
And having got him out of doors is glad.
The like is Joan. But turning home, is sad.
And so is Joan. Oft-times, when Giles doth find
Harsh sights at home, Giles wisheth he were blind.
All this doth Joan. Or that his long-yarned life
Were quite out-spun. The like wish hath his wife.
The children, that he keeps, Giles swears are none
Of his begetting. And so swears his Joan.
In all affections she concurreth still.
If, now, with man and wife, to will, and nill
The selfsame things, a note of concord be:
I know no couple better can agree!

Ben Jonson

Actress

I'd often played the part
on stage
in plays about
the eternal triangle
of mistress husband wife

learning the lines by heart
and speaking them
with true expression
and convincing gesture
movement and well-timed pause

cast always as
'the other woman'
the vulnerable young girl
in scenes of cat and mouse
with the older wife

and yet when she arrived
in brightest turquoise
with a flow of words
about deceit and marriage vows
staged a dramatic scene

I could not answer
uncostumed unmadeup
no bracketed advice on where to move
no scripted words to speak
my character wasn't even written yet

Anne Harvey

Wife to Husband

you are a person
like a tree
standing like rock
moving like water

you show me how
to hold like a root
and how to dance
in a changing rhythm

you hold me close
in a singing stillness
you rock me slow
in a crazy wind

You show me a height
that I may grow to
you cover the sky
with stars and branches

you lose your leaves
without complaining
you know there will be
another spring

you stand like rock
you move like water
you are a person
like a tree

Evangeline Paterson

My Old Dutch

We've been together now for forty years,
An' it don't seem a day too much;
There ain't a lady livin' in the land
As I'd swop for my dear old Dutch.

I calls 'er Sal;
'Er proper name is Sairer;
An' yer may find a gal
As you'd consider fairer.
She ain't a angel – she can start
A-jawin' till it makes yer smart;
She's just a *woman*, bless 'er 'eart,
Is my old gal . . .

We've been together now for forty years,
An' it don't seem a day too much;
There ain't a lady livin' in the land
As I'd swop for my dear old Dutch.

I sees yer, Sal –
Yer pretty ribbons sportin':
Many years now, old gal,
Since them young days of courtin'.
I ain't a coward, still I trust
When we've to part, as part we must,
That Death may come and take me fust
    To wait . . . my pal.

Albert Chevalier

out of Love

First Frost

A girl is freezing in a telephone booth
huddled in her flimsy coat
her face stained by tears
and smeared with lipstick.

She breathes on her thin little fingers.
Fingers like ice. Glass beads in her ears.

She has to beat her way back alone
down the icy street.

First frost. A beginning of losses.
The first frost of telephone phrases.

It is the start of winter glittering on her cheek,
the first frost of having been hurt.

Andrei Voznesensky

She came in from the Frost

She came in from the frost
with her cheeks glowing,
and she filled the room
with a scent of air and perfume,
with her voice ringing
and her utterly work-shattering
chatter.

Immediately she dropped on the carpet
the flat slab of an art magazine
and suddenly it seemed
that in my generous room
was a shortage of space.

This was all a little annoying
not to say silly.
What's more, all at once she wanted
me to read *Macbeth* to her.

Hardly had we got to the 'earth's bubbles',
of which I cannot speak without emotion,
when I noticed that she too was moved
and was staring out of the window.

And there was a big tabby cat
inching its way down the gable
in pursuit of some passionate pigeons.

I was annoyed most of all because
it was not us but the pigeons who were kissing
and that the times of Paolo and Francesca were over.

Alexander Blok

The Lost Mistress

All's over, then: does truth sound bitter
  As one at first believes?
Hark, 'tis the sparrows' good-night twitter
  About your cottage eaves!

And the leaf-buds on the vine are woolly,
  I noticed that, today;
One day more bursts them open fully
  – You know the red turns grey.

Tomorrow we meet the same then, dearest?
  May I take your hand in mine?
Mere friends are we, – well, friends the merest
  Keep much that I resign:

For each glance of the eye so bright and black.
  Though I keep with heart's endeavour, –
Your voice, when you wish the snowdrops back,
  Though it stay in my soul for ever! –

Yet I will but say what mere friends say,
  Or only a thought stronger;
I will hold your hand but as long as all may,
  Or so very little longer!

Robert Browning

from First Love

She:

I don't know why, but something's going wrong –
I felt the point of no return slip by.
Though we're still happy, we still get along

my heart beats like a toneless leaden gong
where once it leapt and raced as if to fly.
I don't know why. But something's going wrong

in me: the spark, the naturalness, has gone –
each day it's getting harder to deny;
though we're still happy, we still get along

I'm out of step. He hasn't changed. How long
each kiss feels with deceit; each touch a lie.
I don't know why, but something's going wrong.

I'd never felt such love – so fierce and strong:
each sight of him, each parting made me cry.
Though we're still happy, we still get along

the love that was to last a whole life long
is coming to an end. No second try,
though we're still happy, we still get along.
I don't know why, but something's going wrong.

He:

I knew it had to come. I couldn't bear
it then; can't take it now. I'll make amends.
I'm willing to agree, now. So – be fair,
there's no need to split up. We'll just be friends.
Like you suggested. Not see quite so much
of each other. Please! I agree. You're right.
I made too much of what we had. Been such
a fool. I'll take the blame. We'll start tonight
– The New Improved Regime. We'll both be free
to do just as we want – the adult way.
I'll do just as you want me to. You'll see.
I'm willing to do anything you say.
I promise. I won't make a scene. Won't cry.
If you'll do just one thing. Don't say goodbye.

Mick Gowar

Hornpipe

Now the peak of summer's past, the sky is overcast
And the love we swore would last for an age seems
   deceit:
Paler is the guelder since the day we first beheld her
In blush beside the elder drifting sweet, drifting sweet.

Oh quickly they fade – the sunny esplanade,
Speed-boats, wooden spades, and the dunes where
   we've lain:
Others will be lying amid the sea-pinks sighing
For love to be undying, and they'll sigh in vain.

It's hurrah for each night we have spent our love so
   lightly.
And never dreamed there might be no more to spend at
   all.
It's goodbye to every lover who thinks he'll live in
   clover
All his life, for noon is over soon and night-dews fall.

If I could keep you there with the berries in your hair
And your lacy fingers fair as the may, sweet may,
I'd have no heart to do it, for to stay love is to rue it
And the harder we pursue it, the faster it's away.

C. Day Lewis

I'm over it now

She whispers

With tears in her lies

Louise Hudson

My cat and i

Girls are simply the prettiest things
My cat and i believe
And we're always saddened
When it's time for them to leave

We watch them titivating
(that often takes a while)
And though they keep us waiting
My cat & i just smile

We like to see them to the door
Say how sad it couldn't last
Then my cat and i go back inside
And talk about the past.

Roger McGough

Mismet

I

       He was leaning by a face,
       He was looking into eyes,
       And he knew a trysting-place,
       And he heard seductive sighs;
           But the face,
           And the eyes,
           And the place,
           And the sighs,
Were not, alas, the right one – the ones meet for him –
Though fine and sweet the features, the feelings all
  abrim.

II

       She was looking at a form,
       She was listening for a tread,
       She could feel a waft of charm
       When a certain name was said;
           But the form
           And the tread,
           And the charm,
           And name said,
Were the wrong ones for her, and ever would be so,
While the heritor of the right it would have saved her
  soul to know!

Thomas Hardy

It's the wrong girl
and the wrong place
Though her face is charming
it's the wrong face.
It's not her face
but it's a lovely face
So it's all right with me . . .

Cole Porter

In the Orchard

'I thought you loved me.' 'No, it was only fun.'
'When we stood there, closer than all?' Well, the
    harvest moon
Was shining and queer in your hair, and it turned my
    head.'
'That made you?' 'Yes.' 'Just the room and the light it
    made
Under the tree?' 'Well, your mouth, too.' 'Yes, my
    mouth?'
'And the quiet there that sang like the drum in the
    booth.
You shouldn't have danced like that.' 'Like what?' 'So
    close,
With your head turned up, and the flower in your hair,
    a rose
That smelt all warm.' 'I loved you. I thought you
    knew
I wouldn't have danced like that with any but you.'
'I didn't know. I thought you knew it was fun.'
'I thought it was love you meant.' 'Well, it's done.'
    'Yes, it's done.
I've seen boys stone a blackbird, and watched them
    drown
A kitten . . . it clawed at the reeds, and they pushed it
    down

Into the pool while it screamed. Is that fun, too?'
'Well, boys are like that . . . Your brothers . . .' 'Yes, I
  know.
But you, so lovely and strong! Not you! Not you!'
'They don't understand it's cruel. It's only a game.'
'And are girls fun, too?' 'No, still in a way it's the
  same.
It's queer and lovely to have a girl . . .' 'Go on.'
'It makes you mad for a bit to feel she's your own,
And you laugh and kiss her, and maybe you give her a
  ring,
But it's only in fun.' 'But I gave you everything.'
'Well, you shouldn't have done it. You know what a
  fellow thinks
When a girl does that.' 'Yes, he talks of her over his
  drinks
And calls her a—' 'Stop that now. I thought you
  knew.'
'But it wasn't with anyone else. It was only you.'
'How did I know? I thought you wanted it too.
I thought you were like the rest. Well, what's to be
  done?'
'To be done?' 'Is it all right?' 'Yes.' 'Sure?' 'Yes, but
  why?'
'I don't know. I thought you were going to cry.
You said you had something to tell me.' 'Yes, I know.
It wasn't anything really . . . I think I'll go.'

'Yes, it's late. There's thunder about, a drop of rain
Fell on my hand in the dark. I'll see you again
At the dance next week. You're sure that everything's
   right?'
'Yes.' 'Well, I'll be going.' 'Kiss me . . .'
   'Good night.' . . .
      'Good night.'

Muriel Stuart

Now I go to films alone
Watch a silent telephone
Send myself a valentine
Whisper softly 'I am mine'

Louise Hudson

Hair Today, No Her Tomorrow

'I've been upstairs,' she said.
'Oh yes?' I said.
'I found a hair,' she said.
'A hair?' I said.
'In the bed,' she said
'From a head?' I said.
'It's not mine,' she said.
'Was it black?' I said.
'It was,' she said.
'I'll explain,' I said.
'You swine,' she said.
'Not quite,' I said.
'I'm going,' she said.
'Please don't,' I said.
'I hate you!' she said.
'You do?' I said.
'Of course,' she said.
'But why?' I said.
'That black hair,' she said.
'A pity,' I said.

'Time for truth,' she said.
'For confessions?' I said.
'Me too,' she said.
'You what?' I said.
'Someone else,' she said.
'Oh dear,' I said.
'So there!' she said.
'Ah well,' I said.
'Guess who?' she said.
'Don't say,' I said.
'I will,' she said.
'You would,' I said.
'Your friend,' she said.
'Oh damn,' I said.
'And his friend,' she said.
'Him too?' I said.
'And the rest,' she said
'Good God,' I said.

'What's that?' she said.
'What's what?' I said.
'That noise?' she said.
'Upstairs?' I said.
'Yes,' she said.
'The new cat,' I said.
'A cat?' she said.
'It's black,' I said.
'Black?' she said.

'Long-haired,' I said.
'Oh no,' she said.
'Oh yes,' I said.
'Oh shit!' she said.
'Goodbye,' I said.

'I lied,' she said.
'You lied?' I said.
'Of course,' she said.
'About my friend?' I said.
'Y-ess,' she said.
'And the others?' I said.
'Ugh,' she said.
'How odd,' I said.
'I'm forgiven?' she said.
'Of course,' I said.
'I'll stay?' she said.
'Please don't,' I said.
'But why?' she said.
'I lied,' I said.
'About what?' she said.
'The new cat,' I said.
'It's white,' I said.

Brian Patten

So We'll Go No More A-Roving

So, we'll go no more a-roving
  So late into the night,
Though the heart be still as loving,
  And the moon be still as bright.

For the sword outwears its sheath,
  And the soul wears out the breast,
And the heart must pause to breathe
  And love itself have rest.

Though the night was made for loving,
  And the day returns too soon,
Yet we'll go no more a-roving
  By the light of the moon.

Lord Byron

Nightsong

So we'll go no more a-raving
So late into the night
Though the heart be still as loving
And the neonsigns so bright

Ate my breakfast egg this morning
playing records from last night
woke to hear the front door closing
as the sky was getting light

No more fish-and-chips on corners
Watching traffic going by
No more branches under streetlamps
No more leaves against the sky

Adrian Henri

from Falling out of Love

When I smile it isn't the same smile now,
when we meet it isn't the same heart beating
   now,
I'm falling out of love.
When I say the things that I used to say,
There's no way to feel what I used to feel
When love was real,
I'm falling out of love.

Herbert Farjeon

Circle

She who is always in my thoughts prefers
Another man, and does not think of me.
Yet he seeks for another's love, not hers;
And some poor girl is grieving for my sake.
   Why then, the devil take
Both her and him; and love; and her; and me.

Bhartrhari

To . . .

When I loved you, I can't but allow
   I had many an exquisite minute;
But the scorn that I feel for you now
   Hath even more luxury in it!

Thus, whether we're on or we're off,
   Some witchery seems to await you;
To love you is pleasant enough,
   But oh! 'tis delicious to hate you!

Thomas Moore

My heart still hovering round about you,
I thought I could not live without you;
Now we have lived three months asunder,
How I lived with you is the wonder.

Robert, Earl Nugent

from A Shropshire Lad

Oh, when I was in love with you,
   Then I was clean and brave,
And miles around the wonder grew
   How well did I behave.

And now the fancy passes by,
   And nothing will remain,
And miles around they'll say that I
   Am quite myself again.

A. E. Housman

Your Little Hands

Your little hands,
Your little feet,
Your little mouth –
Oh, God, how sweet!

Your little nose,
Your little ears,
Your eyes, that shed
Such little tears!

Your little voice,
So soft and kind;
Your little soul,
Your little mind!

Samuel Hoffenstein

Parting

Since there's no help, come let us kiss and
    part, –
Nay I have done, you get no more of me;
And I am glad, yea glad with all my heart,
That thus so cleanly I myself can free;
Shake hands for ever, cancel all our vows,
And when we meet at any time again,
Be it not seen in either of our brows
That we one jot of former love retain.
Now at the last gasp of Love's latest breath,
When, his pulse failing, Passion speechless lies,
When Faith is kneeling by his bed of death,
And Innocence is closing up his eyes, –
Now if thou would'st, when all have given him
    over,
From death to life thou might'st him yet recover!

Michael Drayton

Song for a Beautiful Girl Petrol-Pump Attendant on the Motorway

I wanted your soft verges
but you gave me the hard shoulder.

Adrian Henri

Spellbinding

'I must go,' he says
lips widening
'I know,' she says
grip tightening

'It's time,' he says
heart racing
'It is,' she says
pulse pounding

'We must part,' he says
soul aching
'We must,' she says
spell breaking

Ellen Wilkie

I remember the way we parted.
   The day and the way we met;
You hoped we were both broken-hearted,
   And knew we should both forget.

And the best and the worst of this is
   That neither is most to blame,
If you have forgotten my kisses,
   And I have forgotten your name.

Algernon Swinburne

Fin

I know it's the end.
I can see it coming. I'm
like those women in the cinema who make you mad
    fumbling for gloves
elbowing themselves into coats, buttoning up –
such a final snapping shut of handbags
the minute it looks like it's all over
but a change of mood and music.
So you demand response, do you,
right to the bitter end, you like
to see the credits roll?
I'm off.

Liz Lochhead

Freedom

Now heaven be thanked, I am out of love again!
I have been long a slave, and now am free;
I have been tortured, and am eased of pain;
I have been blind, and now my eyes can see;
I have been lost, and now my way lies plain;
I have been caged, and now I hold the key;
I have been mad, and now at last am sane;
I am wholly I that was but half of me.
So a free man, my dull proud path I plod,
Who, tortured, blind, mad, caged, was once a God.

Jan Struther

Lost Love

Lost Love

His eyes are quickened so with grief,
He can watch a grass or leaf
Every instant grow; he can
Clearly through a flint wall see,
Or watch the startled spirit flee
From the throat of a dead man.
   Across two counties he can hear
And catch your words before you speak.
The woodlouse or the maggot's weak
Clamour rings in his sad ear,
And noise so slight it would surpass
Credence – drinking sound of grass,
Worm talk, clashing jaws of moth
Chumbling holes in cloth;
The groan of ants who undertake
Gigantic loads for honour's sake
(Their sinews creak, their breath comes thin);
Whir of spiders when they spin,
And minute whispering, mumbling, sighs
Of idle grubs and flies.
   This man is quickened so with grief,
He wanders god-like or like thief
Inside and out, below, above,
Without relief seeking lost love.

Robert Graves

from Haiku Sequence

During our argument
a pink rose
tightens its petals.

                After he leaves
                I cry aloud
                to the room

Phone call
his three day stubble
scraping the distance

                Left to the wind
                all the lilies
                and all his lies

In the garbage bin
mound of snow
and a valentine

Alexis Rotella

from Tonight I can Write

Tonight I can write the saddest lines.

Write, for example, 'The night is starry
and the stars are blue and shiver in the distance.'

The night wind revolves in the sky and sings.

Tonight I can write the saddest lines.
I loved her, and sometimes she loved me too.

Though nights like this one I held her in my arms.
I kissed her again and again under the endless sky.

She loved me, sometimes I loved her too.
How could one not have loved her great still eyes.

Tonight I can write the saddest lines.
To think that I do not have her. To feel that I have lost
   her . . .

I no longer love her, that's certain, but how I loved her.
My voice tried to find the wind to touch her hearing.

Another's. She will be another's. As she was before my
   kisses.
Her voice, her bright body. Her infinite eyes.

I no longer love her, that's certain, but maybe I love
   her.
Love is so short, forgetting is so long.

Because through nights like this one I held her in my
   arms
my soul is not satisfied that it has lost her.

Though this be the last pain that she makes me suffer
and these the last verses that I write for her.

Pablo Neruda
(Translated by W. S. Merwin)

from Discordants

Music I heard with you was more than music,
And bread I broke with you was more than bread;
Now that I am without you, all is desolate;
All that was once so beautiful is dead.

Your hands once touched this table and this silver,
And I have seen your fingers hold this glass.
These things do not remember you, beloved,
And yet your touch upon them will not pass.

For it was in my heart you moved among them
And blessed them with your hands and with your eyes;
And in my heart they will remember always
They knew you once, O beautiful and wise.

Conrad Aiken

from In Memoriam

I hold it true, whate'er befall;
   I feel it, when I sorrow most;
   'Tis better to have loved and lost
Than never to have loved at all.

Alfred, Lord Tennyson

Adrian Henri's Talking After Christmas Blues

Well I woke up this mornin' it was Christmas Day
And the birds were singing the night away
I saw my stocking lying on the chair
Looked right to the bottom but you weren't there
there was

> apples
>> oranges
>>> chocolates
>>>> . . . aftershave

– but no you.

So I went downstairs and the dinner was fine
There was pudding and turkey and lots of wine
And I pulled those crackers with a laughing face
Till I saw there was no one in your place
there was

> mince pies
>> brandy
>>> nuts and raisins
>>>> . . . mashed potato

– but no you.

Now it's New Year and it's Auld Lang Syne
And it's 12 o'clock and I'm feeling fine
Should Auld Acquaintance be Forgot?
I don't know girl, but it hurts a lot
there was
        whisky
         vodka
           dry Martini (stirred
             but not shaken)
 . . . and 12 New Year resolutions
– all of them about you.

So it's all the best for the year ahead
As I stagger upstairs and into bed
Then I looked at the pillow by my side
 . . . I tell you baby I almost cried
there'll be
        Autumn
       Summer
      Spring
         . . . and Winter
– all of them without you.

Adrian Henri

The Voice

Woman much missed, how you call to me, call to me,
Saying that now you are not as you were
When you had changed from the one who was all to
   me,
But as at first, when our day was fair.

Can it be you that I hear? Let me view you, then,
Standing as when I drew near to the town
Where you would wait for me: yes, as I knew you then,
Even to the original air-blue gown!

Or is it only the breeze, in its listlessness
Travelling across the wet mead to me here,
You being ever dissolved to wan wistlessness,
Heard no more again far or near?

   Thus I; faltering forward,
   Leaves around me falling,
Wind oozing thin through the thorn from norward,
   And the woman calling.

Thomas Hardy

Absence

I visited the place where we last met.
Nothing was changed, the gardens were
   well-tended,
The fountains sprayed their usual steady jet;
There was no sign that anything had ended
And nothing to instruct me to forget.

The thoughtless birds that shook out of the trees,
Singing an ecstasy I could not share,
Played cunning in my thoughts. Surely in these
Pleasures there could not be a pain to bear
Or any discord shake the level breeze.

It was because the place was just the same
That made your absence seem a savage force,
For under all the gentleness there came
An earthquake tremor: fountain, birds and grass
Were shaken by my thinking of your name.

Elizabeth Jennings

Sonnet

Time does not bring relief; you all have lied
Who told me time would ease me of my pain!
I miss him in the weeping of the rain;
I want him at the shrinking of the tide;
The old snows melt from every mountain-side,
And last year's leaves are smoke in every lane;
But last year's bitter loving must remain
Heaped on my heart, and my old thoughts abide.
There are a hundred places where I fear
To go, – so with his memory they brim.
And entering with relief some quiet place
Where never fell his foot or shone his face
I say, 'There is no memory of him here!'
And so stand stricken, so remembering him.

Edna St Vincent Millay

Simple Lyric

When I think of her sparkling face
And of her body that rocked this way and that,
When I think of her laughter,
Her jubilance that filled me,
It's a wonder I'm not gone mad.

She is away and I cannot do what I want.
Other faces pale when I get close.
She is away and I cannot breathe her in.

The space her leaving has created
I have attempted to fill
With bodies that numbed upon touching,
Among them I expected her opposite,
And found only forgeries.

Her wholeness I know to be fiction of my making,
Still I cannot dismiss the longing for her;
It is a craving for sensation new flesh
Cannot wholly calm or cancel,
It is perhaps for more than her.

At night above the parks the stars are swarming.
The streets are thick with nostalgia;
I move through senseless routine and insensitive chatter
As if her going did not matter.
She is away and I cannot breathe her in.
I am ill simply through wanting her.

Brian Patten

No Loser, No Weeper

'I hate to lose something,'
  then she bent her head
'even a dime, I wish I was dead.
I can't explain it. No more to be said.
Cept I hate to lose something.'

'I lost a doll once and cried for a week.
She could open her eyes, and do all but speak.
I believe she was took, by some doll-snatching-sneak
I tell you, I hate to lose something.'

'A watch of mine once, got up and walked away.
It had twelve numbers on it and for the time of day.
I'll never forget it and all I can say
Is I really hate to lose something.'

'Now if I felt that way bout a watch and a toy,
What you think I feel bout my lover-boy?
I ain't threatening you madam, but he is my evening's joy.
And I mean I really hate to lose something.'

Maya Angelou

Today

saw the last of my Spanish shampoo
lasted an age now that sharing with you
Such a thing of the past is. Giant size
our brand was always a compromise.
My new one's 'tailored exactly to my needs'
nonspill protein rich feeds
body promises to solve my problem hair,
Sweetheart, these days I cannot care.

but oh – oh insomniac moonlight
how unhoneyed is my middle of the night.
Oh I can see
you far enough beyond me
how we'll get back together.
Campsites in Spain moonlight heavy weather
Today saw the end of my Spanish shampoo
    the end of my third month without you.

Liz Lochhead

Song

Stop all the clocks, cut off the telephone,
Prevent the dog from barking with a juicy bone,
Silence the pianos and with muffled drum
Bring out the coffin, let the mourners come.

Let aeroplanes circle moaning overhead
Scribbling on the sky the message He Is Dead,
Put crêpe bows round the white necks of the public doves,
Let the traffic policemen wear black cotton gloves.

He was my North, My South, My East and West,
My working week and my Sunday rest,
My noon, my midnight, my talk, my song;
I thought that love would last for ever: I was wrong.

The stars are not wanted now: put out every one;
Pack up the moon and dismantle the sun;
Pour away the ocean and sweep up the wood.
For nothing now can ever come to any good.

W. H. Auden

I So Liked Spring

I so liked Spring last year
   Because you were here; –
     The thrushes too –
Because it was these you so liked to hear –
     I so liked you.

   This year's a different thing, –
    I'll not think of you.
But I'll like Spring because it is simply Spring
    As the thrushes do.

Charlotte Mew

I get along without you very well,
Of course I do,
Except perhaps in Spring
But I should never think of Spring
For that would surely break
   my heart in two . . .

H. Carmichael

Bredon Hill

In summertime on Bredon
   The bells they sound so clear;
Round both the shires they ring them
   In steeples far and near,
   A happy noise to hear.

Here of a Sunday morning
   My love and I would lie,
And see the coloured counties,
   And hear the larks so high
   About us in the sky.

The bells would ring to call her
   In valleys miles away:
'Come all to church, good people;
   Good people, come and pray.'
   But here my love would stay.

And I would turn and answer
   Among the springing thyme,
'Oh, peal upon our wedding,
   And we will hear the chime,
   And come to church in time.'

But when the snows at Christmas
    On Bredon top were strown,
My love rose up so early
    And stole out unbeknown
    And went to church alone.

They tolled the one bell only,
    Groom there was none to see,
The mourners followed after,
    And so to church went she,
    And would not wait for me.

The bells they sound on Bredon,
    And still the steeples hum.
'Come all to church, good people, –'
    Oh, noisy bells, be dumb;
I hear you, I will come.

A. E. Housman

A Deep-Sworn Vow

Others because you did not keep
That deep-sworn vow have been friends of mine;
Yet always when I look death in the face,
When I clamber to the heights of sleep,
Or when I grow excited with wine,
Suddenly I meet your face.

W. B. Yeats

Remember

Remember me when I am gone away,
Gone far away into the silent land;
When you can no more hold me by the hand,
Nor I half turn to go yet turning stay.
Remember me when no more day by day
You tell me of our future that you plann'd:
Only remember me; you understand
It will be late to counsel then or pray.
Yet if you should forget me for a while
And afterwards remember, do not grieve:
For if the darkness and corruption leave
A vestige of the thoughts that once I had,
Better by far you should forget and smile
Than that you should remember and be sad.

Christina Rossetti

Last Love

A Marriage Ring

The ring so worn as you behold,
So thin, so pale, is yet of gold:
The passion such it was to prove;
Worn with life's cares, love yet was love.

George Crabbe

Her Greatest Love

At sixty she's experiencing
the greatest love of her life.

She walks arm in arm with her lover,
the wind ruffles their grey hairs.

Her lover says:
– You have hair like pearls.

Her children say:
– You silly old fool.

Anna Swirszczynska
(Translated by M. Marshment and G. Baran)

All Souls' Night

My love came back to me
Under the November tree
Shelterless and dim.
He put his hand upon my shoulder,
He did not think me strange or older,
Nor I, him.

Frances Cornford

Autumn

He told his life story to Mrs Courtly
Who was a widow. 'Let us get married shortly,'
He said. 'I am no longer passionate,
But we can have some conversation before it is too
  late.'

Stevie Smith

In a Bath Teashop

'Let us not speak, for the love we bear one another –
  Let us hold hands and look.'
She, such a very ordinary little woman;
  He, such a thumping crook;
But both, for a moment, little lower than the angels
  In the teashop's ingle-nook.

John Betjeman

John Anderson My Jo

John Anderson my jo, John,
   When we were first acquent;
Your locks were like the raven,
   Your bony brow was brent;
But now your brow is bald, John,
   Your locks are like the snaw;
But blessings on your frosty head,
   John Anderson my Jo.

John Anderson my jo, John,
   We clamb the hill the gither;
And mony a jolly day, John,
   We've had wi' ane anither:
Now we maun totter down, John,
   And hand in hand we'll go;
And sleep the gither at the foot,
   John Anderson my Jo.

Robert Burns

Upon The Death of Sir Albert Morton's Wife

He first deceased, she for a little tried
To live without him, liked it not, and died.

Sir Henry Wootton

When You are Old

When you are old and grey and full of sleep,
And nodding by the fire, take down this book,
And slowly read, and dream of the soft look
Your eyes had once, and of their shadows deep;

How many loved your moments of glad grace,
And loved your beauty with love false or true,
But one man loved the pilgrim soul in you,
And loved the sorrows of your changing face;

And bending down beside the glowing bars,
Murmur, a little sadly, how Love fled
And paced upon the mountains overhead
And hid his face amid a crowd of stars.

W. B. Yeats

Here lies the man RICHARD,
    And MARY his wife;
Their surname was PRITCHARD,
    They lived without strife.
And the reason was plain:
    They abounded in riches,
They had no care or pain,
And the wife wore the breeches.

Chelmsford Cathedral, Essex

from To Mary

. . . Thy needles, once a shining store,
For my sake restless heretofore,
Now rust disused, and shine no more,
    My Mary! . . .

Thy silver locks, once auburn bright,
Are still more lovely in my sight
Than golden beams of orient light,
    My Mary! . . .

For, could I view nor them nor thee,
What sight worth seeing could I see?
The sun would rise in vain for me,
    My Mary! . . .

Partakers of thy sad decline,
Thy hands their little force resign:
Yet, gently prest, press gently mine,
    My Mary! . . .

And then I feel that still I hold
A richer store ten thousandfold
Than misers fancy in their gold,
    My Mary! . . .

And still to love, though prest with ill,
In wintry age to feel no chill,
With me is to be lovely still,
    My Mary! . . .

William Cowper

My Dearest Dust

My dearest dust, could not thy hasty day
Afford thy drowszy patience leave to stay
One hower longer: so that we might either
Sate up, or gone to bedd together?
But since thy finisht labor hath possest
Thy weary limbs with early rest,
Enjoy it sweetly: and thy widdowe bride
Shall soone repose her by thy slumbring side.
Whose business, now, is only to prepare
My nightly dress, and call to prayre:
Mine eyes wax heavy and ye day growes old.
The dew falls thick, my belovd growes cold.
Draw, draw ye closed curtaynes: and make
  roome:
My deare, my dearest dust; I come, I come.

Lady Catherine Dyer

Epitaph on the monument to Sir William Dyer
in the parish church of Colmworth in
Bedfordshire, 1641

An Arundel Tomb

Side by side, their faces blurred,
The earl and countess lie in stone,
Their proper habits vaguely shown
As jointed armour, stiffened pleat,
And that faint hint of the absurd –
The little dogs under their feet.

Such plainness of the pre-baroque
Hardly involves the eye, until
It meets his left-hand gauntlet, still
Clasped empty in the other; and
One sees, with a sharp tender shock,
His hand withdrawn, holding her hand.

They would not think to lie so long.
Such faithfulness in effigy
Was just a detail friends would see:
A sculptor's sweet commissioned grace
Thrown off in helping to prolong
The Latin names around the base.

They would not guess how early in
Their supine stationary voyage
The air would change to soundless damage,
Turn the old tenantry away;
How soon succeeding eyes begin
To look, not read. Rigidly they

Persisted, linked through lengths and breadths
Of time. Snow fell, undated. Light
Each summer thronged the glass. A bright
Litter of birdcalls strewed the same
Bone-riddled ground. And up the paths
The endless altered people came,

Washing at their identity.
Now, helpless in the hollow of
An unarmorial age, a trough
Of smoke in slow suspended skeins
Above their scrap of history,
Only an attitude remains:

Time has transfigured them into
Untruth. The stone fidelity
They hardly meant has come to be
Their final blazon, and to prove
Our almost-instinct almost true:
What will survive of us is love.

Philip Larkin

Index of first lines

1 your hair falls in a cock's tail	42
A girl in our village makes love in the churchyard	35
A girl is freezing in a telephone booth	162
A single flow'r he sent me, since we met	105
All's over, then: does truth sound bitter	165
Although I conquer all the earth	83
Although I saw you	41
Among all lovely things my Love had been	99
An orange on the table	82
. . . . and God, bless Carmel Piper	12
At sixty she's experiencing	214
Barbara Cushion	28
Being your slave, what should I do but tend	58
Beloved, thou hast brought me many flowers	104
Black girl black girl	52
Breathless, we flung us on the windy hill	88
'Come, come,' said Tom's father, 'at your time of life	129
Come hither, womankind and all their worth	108
Dave. Dear Dave	74
Did you see me walking by the Buick Repairs?	78
During our argument	193
First time he kissed me, he but only kissed	110
Flipping 'eck, cor blimey, strewth	10
Flowers you cultivate and prize	44
From middle March to April	70
Girls are simply the prettiest things	169

Give me, my love, that billing kiss	114
Go, lovely rose	103
Had we but world enough, and time	53
Have you seen but a bright lily grow	51
He first deceased, she for a little tried	218
He loves me for imagined excellences	32
He told his life story to Mrs Courtly	216
He was leaning by a face	170
He's a fool that marries at Yule	135
Here lies the man RICHARD	220
Here's a happy new year! but with reason	141
His eyes are quickened so with grief	192
Horace and Hattie, in cacophonous concert	151
How do I love thee? Let me count the ways	62
I	40
I am my mammy's ae bairn	130
I can't get enoughsky	26
I carry your heart with me (i carry it in	64
I dare not ask a kisse	111
I don't know why, but something's going wrong	166
I gave them to you	116
I get along without you very well	208
'I hate to lose something,'	205
I have often walked down this street before	76
I hold it true, whate'er befall	197
I know it's the end	188
'I must go,' he says	186
I must not think of thee; and, tired yet strong	86
I ne'er was struck before that hour	30

I remember the way we parted   187

'I saw you take his kiss!' ''Tis true.'   110

I so liked Spring last year   208

I take my pen in hand   119

'I thought you loved me.' 'No, it was only fun.'   172

I visited the place where we last met   201

I wait for you whose half past six is seven   57

I wanted your soft verges   185

I will make you brooches and toys for your delight   98

I wish I could remember that first day   31

I won't send roses or hold the door   106

I wondered by my troth, what thou, and I   94

I would rather eat fish and chips   68

I'd often played the part   155

If one day you would be wed   128

If there be any one can take my place   92

If thou must love me, let it be for nought   50

If you love me, love me true   97

I'm getting married in the morning   135

I'm in a nice bit of trouble, I confess   132

I'm over it now   169

In among the silver birches winding ways of tarmac wander   14

In summertime on Bredon   209

It is to be all made of sighs and tears . . .   3

it may not always be so; and i say   93

It's the wrong girl   171

It was Mabbie without the grammar school gates   17

It was not in the Winter   102

It was what we did not do that I remember   38

The Language of Love 229

'I've been upstairs,' she said 175

Jenny kiss'd me in a dream 113

Jenny kiss'd me when we met 112

John Anderson my jo, John 217

Let me not to the marriage of true minds 139

Let us for this love 80

Let us have winter loving that the heart 89

'Let us not speak, for the love we bear one another 216

Life in a day: he took his girl to the ballet 147

Love and marriage, love and marriage 129

Love comes quietly 91

Love is a circle that doth restless move 3

Love is feeling cold in the back of vans 6

love is more thicker than forget 2

Love me 69

Lying apart now, each in a separate bed 153

Mistress Anne 72

Monday for wealth 135

More than a catbird hates a cat 45

Music I heard with you was more than music 196

My dearest dust, could not thy hasty day 222

My heart still hovering round about you 181

My love came back to me 215

My love is like a cabbage 106

My love will come 81

My true love hath my heart, and I have his 63

'Never shall a young man 49

Not an ounce excessive, not an inch too little 46

Now heaven be thanked, I am out of love again! 189

Now I go to films alone	174
Now the peak of summer's past, the sky is overcast	168
Now what is love, I pray thee tell?	7
O bridesmaid, ere the happy knot was tied	146
O, love, love, love!	5
O my Luve's like a red, red rose	107
O, that joy so soon should waste!	109
Oh I remember how the sea	21
Oh, when I was in love with you	182
Others because you did not keep	211
Ozzie puts his hands in his pockets	24
Pick up the phone before it is too late	55
Remember me when I am gone away	212
Roses are red, my love	104
St Catherine, St Catherine, O lend me thine aid	128
saw the last of my Spanish shampoo	206
She came in from the frost	163
She stood in her scarlet gown	77
She tells her love while half asleep	90
She who is always in my thoughts prefers	180
Side by side, their faces blurred	223
Since there's no help, come let us kiss and part	184
Singing, today I married my white girl	137
So, they have done it. And here they are	79
So we'll go no more a-raving	179
So, we'll go no more a-roving	178
Some keep them in shoeboxes away from the light	126
Some say that love's a little boy	4

Some starry night when her kisses make you tingle 141

Some wed for gold and some for pleasure 144

Stop all the clocks, cut off the telephone 207

Strephon kissed me in the spring 115

Sudden swallows swiftly skimming 134

Sweet, good night! 34

Take my plastic flowers 143

The honeymoon is over 149

The ring so worn as you behold 214

The sky is blue, or something. Anyway, it's there 76

The wedding day appointed was 144

Thelma was a Brownie 20

There were never strawberries 84

This girl 100

This is to let you know 122

This knot I knit 131

this little bride & groom are 142

This one is entering her teens 33

. . . Thy needles, once a shining store 220

Time does not bring relief; you all have lied 202

'Tis easy enough to be twenty-one 133

To change the name, and not the letter 136

Tonight I can write the saddest lines 194

Well I woke up this mornin' it was Christmas Day 198

Were all the peaks of Gwynedd 124

Western wind, when wilt thou blow 82

We've been together now for forty years 159

When I am near you, I'm like a child 68

When I am sad and weary 77

When I loved you, I can't but allow 181

When I smile it isn't the same smile now 180

When I think of her sparkling face 203

When I was in my fourteenth year 19

When you are old and grey and full of sleep 219

When you first combed back your fringe 37

When your face 87

Who else can make me feel like I'm handsome and tall 22

Who says that Giles and Joan at discord be? 154

Why am I dressed in these beautiful clothes? 145

Why doesn't she come? 59

Why have such scores of lovely, gifted girls 140

Woman much missed, how you call to me, call to me 200

Woman to man, they lie 66

Yes: I perceive it's to your Love 117

Yes, yours, my love, is the right human face 48

you are a person 157

You ask for a poem 96

You're like the jolliest picnic in a children's book 43

You're the top, you're the Coliseum 42

Your dressing, dancing, gadding, where's the good in? 136

Your little hands 183

Your white skin and my brown skin 65

Index of authors

Abse, Dannie   137

Adams, Franklin P.   113

Aiken, Conrad   196

Amichai, Yehuda   116

Angelou, Maya   205

Astbury, Anthony   68

Aubrey, John   131

Auden, W. H.   4, 207

Berry, James   74

Betjeman, John   14, 216

Bhartrhari   180

Blok, Alexander   163

Bosley, Keith   42

Brooke, Rupert   88

Brooks, Gwendolyn   17

Browning, Elizabeth Barrett   50, 62, 104, 110

Browning, Robert   165

Burn, Michael   124

Burns, Robert   107, 130, 217

Bullett, Gerald   19

Byron, Lord,   141, 178

Cahn, S.   129, 141

Carmichael, H.   208

Chevalier, Albert   159

Clare, John   30

Collins, Charles   145

Cope, Wendy   55

Cornford, Frances   215

Coward, Noel   122

Cowper, William   220

Crabbe, George   214

Creeley, Robert   91

cummings, e e   2, 64, 93, 142

Dehn, Paul   112

Donne, John   94

Drayton, Michael   184

Duffy, Carol Ann   126

Dyer, Lady Catherine   222

Ewart, Gavin   43

Farjeon, Herbert   180

Garner, Alan   35

Gowar, Mick   166

Graves, Robert   90, 140, 192

Hamyln, Susan   65

Hardy, Thomas   117, 170, 200

Harvey, Anne 155

Henri, Adrian 6, 179, 185, 198

Herbert, A. P. 59

Herbert, Lord Edward, of Cherbury
    108

Herman, Jerry 22, 106

Herrick, Robert 3, 111

Hoffenstein, Samuel 183

Hogg, James 5

Hood, Thomas 102

Housman, A. E. 182, 209

Hudson, Louise 169, 174

Hunt, Leigh 112

Jennings, Elizabeth 38, 89, 153, 201

Jonson, Ben 51, 109, 154

Joseph, M. K. 100

Larkin, Philip 223

Latham, John 12

Leigh, Fred W. 132, 145

Leonard, Tom 76

Lerner, A. J. 76, 135

Lewis, C. Day 168

Lochhead, Liz 188, 206

Macaig, Norman 46

McGough, Roger 169

McGrath, Tom 80

MacNeice, Louis 148

Marvell, Andrew 53

Masuhito 41

Mew, Charlotte 208

Meynell, Alice 86

Millay, Edna St Vincent 202

Millward, Eric 32, 79

Mitchell, Adrian 77

Mole, John 10

Moore, Thomas 114, 129, 181

Morgan, Edwin 84

Muir, Edwin 48

Nash, Ogden 33, 45

Neruda, Pablo 194

Nilsen, Bjorn 143

Nugent, Earl Robert 181

O'Hara, Frank 78

Owen, Gareth 21

Parker, Dorothy 105

Patmore, Coventry 110

Patten, Brian 96, 175, 203

Paterson, Evangeline 157

Porter, Cole 42, 171

Prevert, Jacques 82

Raleigh, Sir Walter 7

Randall, Dudley 52

Riddell, Elizabeth   119

Ross, Alan   66

Rossetti, Christina   23, 92, 212

Rotella, Alexis   193

Scannell, Vernon   20

Shakespeare, William   3, 34, 58, 139

Sidgwick, Frank   40

Sidney, Sir Philip   63

Skelton, John   72

Smith, Stevie   216

Stevenson, Robert Louis   98

Struther, Jan   189

Stuart, Muriel   172

Swinburne, Algernon   187

Swirszczynska, Anna   214

Teasdale, Sara   115

Tennyson, Alfred, Lord   146, 197

Tessimond, A. S. J.   57

Toson, Shimazaki   37

Viorst, Judith   26, 149

Voznesensky, Andrei   162

Waller, Edmund   103

Warner, Sylvia Townsend   28

Weaver, Barry   24

Wickham, Anna   68

Wilkie, Ellen   186

Wine, Marian   69

Wootton, Sir Henry   218

Wordsworth, William   99

Wright, Kit   151

Yeats, W. B.   49, 211, 219

Yevtushenko, Yevgeny   81, 87

Acknowledgements

The author and the publisher would like to thank the following for their kind permission to reprint copyright material in this book:

Anthony Sheil Associates Ltd and Dannie Abse for 'Epithalamion' Copyright © Dannie Abse 1952, first published by Hutchison in *Walking Under Water*; Doubleday for 'Jenny Kiss'd Me in a Dream' from *So Much Velvet* by Franklin P. Adams. Copyright © 1924 by Doubleday, a division of Bantam Doubleday Dell Publishing Group, Inc. Reprinted by permission of the publisher; Oxford University Press, Inc for an extract from 'Discordants' from *Collected Poems* by Conrad Aiken. Copyright © 1953, 1970 by Conrad Aiken; renewed 1981 by Mary Aiken; Abner Stein for 'Gifts of Love' by Yehuda Amichai; The Virago Press for 'No Loser, No Weeper' by Maya Angelou; Only Publications for 'Gourmet' by Anthony Astbury from *The Two of Us*; Faber and Faber Ltd for 'O Tell Me the Truth About Love' and 'Song: Stop All The Clocks' from *Collected Poems* by W. H. Auden; Hamish Hamilton Ltd for 'Teach the Making of Summer' from *When I Dance* by James Berry. Copyright © 1988 by James Berry; Eyre and Spottiswoode Ltd for 'She Came in from the Frost' by Alexander Blok; W. H. Allen for 'I Love You Because' from *The War Wife* by Keith Bosley; Gwendolyn Brooks for 'The Ballad of Chocolate Mabbie' from *The World of Gwendolyn Brooks*; A. D. Peters for 'First Love' by Gerald Bullett. Reprinted by permission of Peters, Fraser & Dunlop Ltd; Chatto and Windus for 'Welsh Love Letter' by Michael Burn from *Open Day and Night* 1978; Hal Shaper Ltd for 'Love and Marriage' and 'The Tender Trap' by Sammy Cahn and J. Van Heusen published by Hal Shaper Ltd, London; Chappell Music Ltd for 'I Get Along Without You Very Well' by Carmichael/JB Copyright © Famous Music; Faber and Faber Ltd for 'Message' from *Making Cocoa for Kingsley Amis* by Wendy Cope; Christopher Cornford for 'All Souls Night' by Frances Cornford; Methuen London for 'This is to Let You

by Peterloo Poets, 1982; Canongate Publishing Ltd for 'Words' by Tom Leonard from *Scottish Love Poems*; Chappell Music Ltd for 'On the Street Where You Live' and 'Get Me to the Church on Time' by Lerner/Loewe, Copyright © Chappell & Co Inc; Jonathan Cape Ltd on behalf of the Executors of the Estate of C. Day Lewis for 'Hornpipe' from *Collected Poems*, 1954, published by the Hogarth Press and Jonathan Cape Ltd; Liz Lochhead for 'Fin'; Canongate Publishing Ltd for 'Today' by Liz Lochhead from *Scottish Love Poems*; Chatto and Windus on behalf of Norman MacCraig for 'True Ways' from *Collected Poems*; Jonathan Cape Ltd for 'My Cat and I' by Roger McGough from *The Mersey Sound*; Canongate Publishing Ltd for 'Paradox' by Tom McGrath from *Scottish Love Poems*; Faber and Faber Ltd for 'Les Sylphides' from *The Collected Poems of Louis MacNeice*; Charles Scitbner's sons for 'I Like You' by Masuhito from *I Like You and Other Poems*; The Estate of Edna St Vincent Millay for 'Time Does Not Bring Relief; You Have All Lied' from *Collected Sonnets*, Revised and Expanded Edition, Harper & Row, 1988. Copyright 1917, 1945 by Edna St Vincent Millay. Reprinted by permission; Peterloo Poets for 'All Change' from *Appropriate Names* by Eric Millward published by Peterloo Poets, 1987, and for 'The Girl's Confession' from *Dead Letters* by Eric Millward published by Peterloo Poets, 1978; W. H. Allen for 'Celia, Celia' by Adrian Mitchell from *The Apeman Cometh* published by Allison & Busby; Peterloo Poets for 'Taking the Plunge' from *Boo to a Goose* by John Mole published by Peterloo Poets, 1987; Carcanet Press Ltd for 'Strawberries' by Edwin Morgan from *Poets of Thirty Years*; Faber and Faber Ltd for 'The Confirmation' from *The Collected Poems of Edwin Muir*; Andre Deutsch Ltd for 'To My Valentine' and 'The Romantic Age' by Ogden Nash from *I Wouldn't Have Missed It*; Jonathan Cape Ltd on behalf of the Estate of Pablo Neruda for an extract from 'Tonight I Can Write' from *Twenty Love Poems and A Song of Despair* translated by W. S. Merwin; Hamish Hamilton Ltd for 'Take My Plastic Flowers' by Bjorn Nilsen from *A World of Love*; City Lights Books Inc for 'Song' by Frank O'Hara; William Collins

Ltd for 'Salcombe' from *Song of the City* by Gareth Owen; Gerald Duckworth and Co Ltd for 'One Perfect Rose' by Dorothy Parker; Unwin Hyman Ltd for 'Simple Lyric', 'Hair Today No Her Tomorrow' and 'A Blade of Grass' by Brian Patten from *Storm Damage*, 1988 and *Love Poems*, 1984 published by Unwin Hyman Ltd; Taxus and Stride Publications for 'Wife to Husband' by Evangeline Paterson; Chappell Music Ltd for 'You're the Top' by Cole Porter, Copyright © Harms Inc and 'It's All Right With Me' by Cole Porter, Copyright © Buxton Hill Music; Laurence Pollinger Ltd on behalf of New Directions Publishing Corporation for 'Alicante' by Jacques Prevert from *Paroles*, published by Penguin Book Ltd; Angus and Robertson for 'The Letter' by Elizabeth Riddell from *Forbears,* Copyright © Elizabeth Riddell 1961; Alan Ross for 'In Bloemfontein' from *Coastwise Lights* published by Collins Harvill; Simon & Schuster for 'Haiku Sequence' by Alexis Rotella from *The Haiku Anthology* edited by Cor Van Den Heuvel; Robson Books for 'Thelma' by Vernon Scannell from *Funeral Games*; Sidgwick & Jackson Ltd for 'The Aeronaut to his Lady' by Frank Sidgwick from *More Verse*; James MacGibbon as executor of the Literary Estate of Stevie Smith for 'Autumn' from *The Collected Poems of Stevie Smith* (Penguin Modern Classics); Weidenfeld & Nicolson Ltd for 'Freedom' by Jan Struther from *A Time for Lovers*; Jonathan Cape Ltd on behalf of the Estate of Muriel Stuart for 'In the Orchard' from *Selected Poems*; Chatto and Windus for 'Her Greatest Love' by Anna Swirszczynskal; Whiteknights Press for 'Warning to Gloria' by A. S. J. Tessimond from *Collected Poems*, 1986; University of Queensland Press for 'First Love' by Shimazaki Toson translated by James Kirkup from *Modern Japanese Poetry* published by University of Queensland Press; Angus and Robertson for 'The Honeymoon' by Judith Viorst; Lescher & Lescher Ltd for 'The Lizzie Pitofsky Poem', copyright © 1981 by Judith Viorst from *If I Were In Charge of the World and Other Worries* published by Atheneum; Carcanet Press Ltd for 'Blue Eyes' by Sylvia Townsend Warner from *Collected Poems* edited by Claire Harman; Barry Weaver for 'A Puddle in the Life of Oscar Summerfield'; The Virago Press for 'The Little Language' by

Anna Wickham from *Collected Poems and Prose*; Ellen Wilkie for 'Spellbinding'; Nadia Christensen for 'Love Me' by Maria Wine, translated by Nadia Christensen; Century Hutchinson Ltd for 'Hardly Believable Horace and Hattie in Hell' from *Poems 1974–1983* by Kit Wright; Penguin Books for 'Waiting' and 'Colours' by Yevgeny Yevtushenko from *Yevtushenko: Selected Poems* translated by Robin Milner-Gulland and Peter Levi, S. J. (Penguin Books, 1962), copyright © Robin Milner-Gulland and Peter Levi, 1962.